映画の料理

CUISINE ON SCREEN

**60 Famous Japanese Recipes
from 30 Cult Movies**

映画の料理

Sachiyo Harada

CUISINE ON SCREEN

60 Famous Japanese Recipes from 30 Cult Movies

Photography: David Bonnier
Food styling: Sarah Vasseghi

Prestel
Munich · London · New York

Table of Contents

映画の料理

Basics

Yields 2½ cups (600 ml)
Preparation time: 10 minutes
Cooking time: 5 minutes
Resting time: 2 hours

Ingredients

- 4-inch (10-cm) piece kombu (dried kelp)
- 1½ cups (20 g) katsuobushi (dried bonito flakes)
- 2½ cups (600 ml) water

Dashi Broth

1. Add the water and kombu to a saucepan. Let soak for 1 to 2 hours. Put the pan over medium-low heat and bring to almost boiling. Turn off the heat and remove the kombu. Add the katsuobushi and remove from the heat. Let steep for 5 minutes. Filter the broth through a conical strainer.

2. For instant dashi, you can use instead 2 teaspoons instant dashi granules or 2½ teaspoons dashi powder dashi powder added to 2½ cups (600 ml) water.

Serves 4
Preparation time: 3 minutes
Cooking time: 15 minutes
Resting time: 1 hour 10 minutes

Ingredients

- 2¼ cups (450 g) Japanese short-grain (sushi) white rice
- 2¾ cups (660 ml) water

Steamed Rice

1. Prepare the rice. In a bowl, wash the rice under cold running water, stirring it with your hand, then quickly discard the water. Repeat the operation until the water turns completely clear. Drain the rice, put it into a large saucepan, and add the water for cooking. Let stand for about 1 hour, until the rice turns white (it will be translucent at first).

2. Cover the pan with a lid, put it over high heat, and bring to a boil, then let cook for about 3 minutes.* Reduce the heat to low and let simmer for 10 minutes. Remove from the heat and let rest for 10 minutes with the lid on* to let the rice finish cooking in its own steam.

3. Stir with a wet wooden spatula.

* Set a timer—it is practical for cooking.

* The lid is important to prevent steam from escaping, otherwise the rice will dry out.

* Freezing: While the rice is still hot, divide it into four equal servings, wrap it in plastic wrap (clingfilm), and gently flatten. Let cool to room temperature, then freeze. Thaw in a 1,000 W microwave for about 3 minutes.

映画の料理

Fritters and
Dumplings

Serves 4
Preparation time: 15 minutes
Cooking time: 10 minutes
Resting time: 20 minutes

Ingredients

- 3 cups (750 ml) vegetable oil, for frying
- 4 boneless, skin-on chicken thighs or 4 chicken breasts
- 1 cup (125 g) potato starch or cornstarch (cornflour) or all-purpose (plain) flour
- 1 lemon

For the marinade
- ¼ cup (60 ml) soy sauce
- ¼ cup (60 ml) cooking sake
- ⅜ teaspoon black pepper
- 2 cloves garlic, grated
- 1 tablespoon grated ginger

Karaage

1. Make the marinade. Put the soy sauce, sake, and pepper into a bowl. Add the grated garlic and ginger.

2. Cut the chicken thighs into 1¼ to 1½-inch (3–4 cm) pieces and add to the marinade. Cover the bowl and refrigerate for about 20 minutes.

3. Heat the oil in a deep fryer to 320°F (160°C); fine bubbles will appear at this temperature when you dip slightly damp chopsticks into the oil. Remove the chicken pieces from the marinade, drain, and dredge in plenty of potato starch.

4. Deep-fry the chicken pieces for 5 minutes, until golden brown. Drain the excess oil on (kitchen) paper towels and set aside while cooking the remaining pieces. Divide among plates and serve with lemon wedges.

Serves 4
Preparation time: 5 minutes
Resting time: 15 minutes
Cooking time: 30 minutes

These chicken wings make an ideal snack to be eaten with your fingers and enjoyed without moderation.

[Midnight Diner]

Ingredients

- 12 chicken wings
- ½ cup (60 g) cornstarch (cornflour) or potato starch
- 2 to 3 cups (500–750 ml) neutral frying oil (vegetable, canola/rapeseed, etc.)
- 1 lemon, to garnish

For the marinade
- 3 tablespoons soy sauce
- 2 tablespoons cooking sake
- 3½ tablespoons (20 g) grated ginger
- 1 pinch freshly ground black pepper

Tebasaki Karaage

Deep-Fried Chicken Wings

1. Put the chicken wings into a plastic bag and add the soy sauce, sake, ginger, and pepper. Mix the marinade ingredients, knead into the chicken, and let marinate for about 15 minutes. You can replace the soy sauce and sake with 5 tablespoons teriyaki sauce.

2. Remove the chicken wings from the marinade and let drain. Put the cornstarch into a bowl, dredge the wings, and remove the excess.

3. Heat the frying oil to 340°F (170°C) in a cast iron pot or deep fryer over medium-high heat (then reduce to medium heat to keep the temperature steady). Using chopsticks (rinsed first and wiped dry), mix the oil and check the temperature; medium bubbles (like those in champagne) should appear at 340°F (170°C).

4. Deep-fry the chicken wings (about four at a time) for 8 to 10 minutes, until golden brown.

5. When crispy and cooked through, drain on a rack or (kitchen) paper towels.

6. Arrange on plates and serve with a lemon wedge.

This quick and easy recipe can be made using ready-to-use tempura flour or a home-made tempura batter made with regular flour.

[Tempura]

Shrimp Tempura

Ingredients

- 12 raw shrimp (prawns)
- 3 cups (750 ml) vegetable oil, for frying
- 1 pinch salt

For the tempura batter
- ¾ cup (100 g) all-purpose (plain) flour, plus extra for the shrimp (prawns)
- 1 egg
- ⅔ cup (150 ml) cold water

For the tempura dipping sauce
- 1⅔ cups (400 ml) Dashi Broth (see page 9)
- 3 tablespoons mirin
- 3 tablespoons soy sauce

Equipment
- Cast iron pot or skillet

1. For a crispy result, chill all the tempura batter ingredients and bowls in the refrigerator until you are ready to make it.

2. Make the tempura dipping sauce. Put all the ingredients into a small saucepan, bring to a boil, then remove from the heat. Set aside.

3. Peel all the shrimp, leaving on the tail and last section, then cut a slit along the back and remove the black vein. To prevent curling when cooked, make a few thin cuts along the underside of the shrimp, then gently bend and pull to cut the nerve.

4. Sift the flour into a bowl. In another bowl, whisk the egg with the water, then add to the bowl with the flour. Mix briskly with chopsticks, without overmixing the batter (to prevent it from becoming too sticky).

5. Heat the frying oil to 350°F (180°C). Fine bubbles (like in champagne) will appear at this temperature when you dip slightly damp chopsticks into the oil.

6. Dust the shrimp with flour. Using chopsticks, dip three to four shrimp in the tempura batter and deep-fry until crispy. Drain away any excess oil by holding the shrimp vertically over paper (kitchen) towels. Repeat the operation for the remaining shrimp.

7. Heat the dipping sauce and divide among four bowls. Serve the shrimp tempura on small plates, sprinkled with just a little salt or dipped in the sauce.

Toilet

Naoko Ogigami—2010

After their mother's death, three Canadian siblings are forced to live with each other to take care of their grandmother, newly arrived from her native Japan. Ray, a geeky engineer whose rule is never to get close to anyone or feel any emotion, has his life turned upside down by having to share a house with his older brother, Maury, a former pianist who is experiencing depression and now lives as a recluse, and their sister, Lisa, a college student who has always looked down on the people around her. And because their grandmother speaks not a single word of English, family ties are going to prove difficult to forge, at first. This movie, winner of the Toronto Award, is at once moving, warm, and quirky, and runs at a slow and soothing pace. It has a large number of subplots, some of which are left unresolved, but they are always lead us to reflect on compassion for family and the bonds we form with those closest to us—whom we sometimes misunderstand.

Spirited Away

Hayao Miyazaki—2001

For almost twenty years, this animated movie has been the most successful production in the history of Japanese cinema, the winner of both an Oscar and a Golden Bear. One of the director's most traditional and accomplished works, it immerses us in a Japan rich in beliefs, folklore, and traditions. Ten-year-old Chihiro is traveling by car with her parents to their new home. During a stop at what they imagine to be a disused amusement park, she explores the place while her parents gorge themselves on food, only to discover when she returns to them at nightfall that they have turned into pigs. This is the start of a long adventure to escape the spirit world she has just entered, rescue her family and return to her normal life. In order to do this, Chihiro has to confront the terrible witch Yubaba. In order to do this, Chihiro has to confront the terrible witch Yubaba. This magnificent fantasy film seamlessly blends the real and the supernatural in the great tradition of Shinto, Japan's millenary polytheistic religion in which its deities, the spirits of nature known as *kami*, populate the everyday world of the living.

Makes 20
Preparation time: 45 minutes
Cooking time: 15 minutes
Resting time: 40 minutes

Adapted from the Chinese dumplings known as jiaozi, this famous Japanese version of the pot sticker, which became popular after World War II, is both soft and crispy at the same time.

[Toilet]

Ingredients

- 1 tablespoon vegetable oil
- ⅔ cup (150 ml) hot water

For the wrappers
- ⅓ cup (90 ml) lukewarm water
- 1 pinch salt
- 1 cup (130 g) cake (Italian "00") flour
- ⅓ cup plus 1 tablespoon (50 g) all-purpose (plain) flour

For the filling
- 7 ounces (200 g) napa (Chinese) cabbage or pointed cabbage
- 1 teaspoon salt
- ½ (40 g) leek
- 1¾ ounces (50 g) shiitake or white mushrooms
- 5¼ ounces (150 g) sausage meat
- 3 cloves (10 g) garlic, grated
- 1 tablespoon soy sauce
- 1 tablespoon sesame oil
- 1 tablespoon cooking sake (optional)
- 3½ tablespoons (20 g) grated ginger
- Freshly ground black pepper

To serve
- Soy sauce
- Rice vinegar
- Layu (Japanese chili oil, optional)

Gyozas

1. Make the wrappers. Put the water into a bowl, dissolve the salt, and mix with the flours. Knead the dough until smooth. Gather into a ball, cover with plastic wrap (clingfilm), and let rest for 10 minutes. Knead the dough again for about 5 minutes, then let rest at room temperature (in a cool place in summer) for 30 minutes. Roll the dough into a cylindrical shape and cut into 20 slices. On a floured cutting (chopping) board, roll out each piece to a thickness of 1/16 inch (2 mm) and cut into disks with a 4-inch (10-cm) diameter cookie (biscuit) cutter.

2. Make the filling. Mince (very finely chop) the cabbage, sprinkle it with the salt, and let degorge for 20 minutes. Rinse under running water in a strainer, then transfer to a cloth and wring well. Mince the leek and mushrooms. Mix together the vegetables, sausage meat, and garlic, then season the mixture with soy sauce, sesame oil, ginger, sake if using, and pepper. Place 1 tablespoon of the filling in the center of each wrapper and moisten around the edges, then fold in half and crimp to seal, making three to five pleats.

3. Heat 1 tablespoon vegetable oil in a skillet and fry the dumplings for 2 to 3 minutes. Add ⅔ cup (150 ml) hot water and cover with a lid. Cook over medium heat for 10 minutes. Remove the lid and let all the water evaporate.

4. Serve with soy sauce, rice vinegar, and layu.

Serves 4
Preparation time: 30 minutes
Resting time: 20 minutes
Cooking time: 20 minutes

Chihiro, the protagonist of Spirited Away, eats anman, *these small steamed buns filled with* anko, *red bean paste, to regain her strength after her emotional encounter with the witch Yubaba. A real treat!*

[Spirited Away]

Ingredients

- 1⅔ cups (200 g) all-purpose (plain) flour
- 2 teaspoons active dry (fast-action dried) yeast
- ⅓ cup plus 1 tablespoon (90 ml) hot water
- 1½ tablespoons (20 g) superfine (caster) sugar
- 4 teaspoons (20 ml) vegetable oil
- 1 pinch salt
- ½ cup (160 g) anko (sweet red bean/adzuki/azuki paste)

Steamed Buns

1. Sift the flour and yeast into a bowl.
2. Add the hot water, sugar, oil, and salt. Mix with a fork. Knead the dough inside the bowl by hand for a few minutes, then gather into a ball. Cover with plastic wrap (clingfilm) and let rest for 30 minutes.
3. Shape the red bean paste into four small balls.
4. Divide the dough into four equal portions. Gather into small balls, then roll out into disks about 4¾ inches (12 cm) in diameter.
5. Place a bean paste ball in the middle of a dough disk. Gather up the edges and shape into a smooth ball. Repeat the operation with the remaining disks and bean paste.
6. Place the buns on parchment (baking) paper inside a steam basket and steam over high heat for about 20 minutes.

映画の料理 Fritters and Dumplings

Little Forest

Junichi Mori—Summer/Autumn (2014), Winter/Spring (2015)

In the first installment of this two-part movie, *Summer/Autumn*, we see Ichiko return to her hometown, the remote mountain village of Komori, or "little forest," after living in a big city. There she rediscovers the rhythm of nature and what it means to farm the land and live self-sufficiently from the healthy seasonal produce that she prepares with the greatest care and delight. In the second part, *Winter/Spring*, Ichiko is put to the test by the arrival of winter, with its harsh weather and the thick snow that blankets the surrounding area. The reawakening of nature a few months later and the coming of spring lead to a decision to profoundly change her way of life. This film adaptation of the manga by Daisuke Igarashi is a beautiful hymn to nature in which a selection of truly mouthwatering dishes in tune with the four seasons are lovingly, serenely, and poetically presented. It is an ode to a gentle life that brings with it the simple joys of authentic flavors.

Serves 4
Preparation time: 20 minutes
Cooking time: 15 minutes

To keep the tempura as light as possible, the batter must not become sticky.

[Little Forest]

Vegetable Tempura

Ingredients

- 1 bunch asparagus or 1 head puntarelle
- 3½ ounces (100 g) morels or shiitake mushrooms
- All-purpose (plain) flour
- Salt, for serving
- 3 cups (750 ml) vegetable oil, for frying

For the tempura batter
- ¾ cup (100 g) all-purpose (plain) flour
- 1 egg
- ⅔ cup (150 ml) cold water
- 1 pinch salt

For the tempura dipping sauce
- 1⅔ cups (400 ml) Dashi Broth (see page 9)
- 3 tablespoons mirin
- 3 tablespoons soy sauce or teriyaki sauce

Equipment
- Dutch oven (cast iron casserole) or skillet (frying pan)

1. Chill all ingredients and bowls for making the tempura batter in the refrigerator until you are ready to make the batter for a crispy result.

2. To make the tempura dipping sauce, combine the dashi, mirin, and soy sauce in a small saucepan, bring to a boil, then remove from the heat. Set aside.

3. Wash the asparagus spears and cut them diagonally into 2½-inch (6 cm) lengths. Clean the mushrooms.

4. To make the tempura batter, sift the flour into a bowl and add the salt. In another bowl, whisk the egg with the water, then add to the bowl with the flour. Mix briefly with chopsticks, without overmixing the batter to prevent it from becoming too sticky.

5. Heat the frying oil to 340°F (170°C). Champagne-like bubbles will appear at this temperature when you dip slightly damp chopsticks into the oil.

6. Dust the asparagus and mushrooms with flour. Using chopsticks, dip the vegetables into the tempura batter and deep-fry for 3 minutes. Drain the tempura on (kitchen) paper towels.

7. To enjoy, dip the tempura into the sauce, served in a small individual bowl, or into salt on a small plate.

Unlike the previous recipe, where the vegetables are deep-fried individually, here they are cut into pieces, combined, and held together by the batter.

[Little Forest]

Ingredients

- 4 outer leaves pointed cabbage
- All-purpose (plain) flour
- 2 cups (500 ml) vegetable oil, for frying
- Sea salt

For the kakiage batter
- 1¼ cups (150 g) cake (Italian "00") flour
- ⅔ cup (150 ml) water
- 1 egg

Equipment
- Cast-iron casserole or skillet

Cabbage Kakiage

1. Cut the cabbage leaves into small pieces.
2. To make the kakiage batter, sift the flour into a bowl. In another bowl, whisk the egg with the cold water. Make a well in the flour, then add the egg mixture and mix briefly with chopsticks or a fork.
3. Put one-fifth of the cabbage into a separate bowl and lightly dust with about 1 teaspoon flour, then add 4 tablespoons of the kariage batter and mix.
4. Heat the frying oil to 340°F (170°C). Check the temperature by dipping in chopsticks: medium champagne-like bubbles should appear at this temperature.
5. Gather the cabbage mixture into a small patty on a spatula or in a ladle, then use chopsticks or a fork to slide the mixture into the oil. Deep-fry for about 2 minutes, then turn and cook until crispy. Remove, shake off the excess oil, and let drain on a wire rack or (kitchen) paper towels. Repeat the process until all the cabbage mixture is used.
6. Serve with sea salt.

映画の料理

Soups,
Stews, and
Noodles

This is a variant of one of the many Japanese stews, known as nabemono, *or simply* nabe. *Tasty and simmered to perfection.*

[Samurai Gourmet]

Oden

Stewed Radishes, Eggs, Konjac

Ingredients

- 8¾ ounces (250 g) konjac (yam cake)
- ½ daikon (Japanese radish)
- 1¼ pounds (600 g) firm tofu
- 4 hard-boiled eggs
- 4 medium tomatoes, blanched and peeled

For the oden broth
- 6¾ cups (1.6 liters) Dashi Broth (see page 9)

For the broth seasoning
- ¼ cup (60 ml) soy sauce
- ¼ cup (60 ml) mirin
- 1 tablespoon sugar
- ¼ teaspoon salt or to taste

For the miso sauce
- 3½ tablespoons (60 g) white (shiro) miso paste
- 3 tablespoons mirin
- 2½ tablespoons (30 g) sugar

For serving
- Karashi (Japanese mustard)

Equipment
- Casserole or cooking pot

1. To make the miso sauce, put the miso paste into a small saucepan and add the mirin and sugar. Place over medium heat and bring to almost boiling, stirring constantly, then remove from the heat. The sauce should be creamy. Transfer to a container and cover with plastic wrap (clingfilm).

2. Cut the konjac into thirds, then halve horizontally and again diagonally. In a casserole, bring water to a boil, add the konjac and cook for 2 to 3 minutes. Drain. Peel and slice the daikon into 1¼-inch (3 cm)-thick rounds. Cut the tofu into large chunks.

3. Add the dashi and all the broth seasonings to a casserole or earthenware cooking pot and mix to combine. Add the daikon and konjac, bring to a boil, then reduce the heat to medium. Let simmer for about 45 minutes. Add the eggs, tofu, and whole tomatoes. Continue to simmer for about 15 minutes.

4. At the table, serve the oden into small bowls from the pot, adding miso sauce or karashi as desired.

This refreshing and easy-to-make dish is part of the Japanese take on Chinese cuisine, known as chuka *cuisine.*

[The Garden of Words]

Serves 4
Preparation time: 10 minutes
Cooking time: 13 minutes

Ingredients

- 4 small tomatoes
- 2 small cucumbers
- 14 ounces (400 g) ramen noodles
- 4 hard-boiled eggs
- 7 ounces (200 g) canned tuna in oil

For the sauce
- 6 tablespoons teriyaki sauce
- 2 tablespoons water
- 2 tablespoons rice vinegar
- 1 tablespoon sesame oil

Cold Ramen

1. Combine all the sauce ingredients in a small bowl and set aside.
2. Halve the tomatoes. Thinly slice the cucumbers into rounds.
3. Halve the hard-boiled eggs. Drain the tuna.
4. Cook the noodles according to the package directions, then drain and rinse under cold water. Drain again. Divide among four plates. Add all the ingredients to the noodles and pour over the sauce.

One of the quickest ramen noodle soups to make at home, with stir-fried pork and vegetables.

[Midnight Diner]

x

Serves 4
Preparation time: 15 minutes
Cooking time: 15 minutes

Tan Men
Vegetable Ramen

Ingredients

- 4 fresh shiitake or button mushrooms
- 2 scallions (spring onions)
- 4–5 leaves napa (Chinese) cabbage
- ½ carrot
- 1 cup (100 g) bean sprouts
- 2 tablespoons vegetable oil
- 3½ ounces (100 g) pork belly
- 2 tablespoons cooking sake
- 1 tablespoon toasted sesame oil
- 11¼ ounces (320 g) store-bought fresh or dried ramen noodles
- Salt and pepper

For the ramen broth
- 6¾ cups (1.6 liters) hot water
- 4 tablespoons instant ramen soup base

1. To make the broth, dilute the instant ramen soup base with the water in a medium saucepan. Stir, bring to a boil, and set aside.

2. Mince (very finely chop) the mushrooms. Slice the scallions into 2-inch (5-cm) lengths. Cut the cabbage leaves into small pieces. Peel and cut the carrot into thin strips. Wash the bean sprouts.

3. Fill a pot or large casserole with water to cook the noodles and bring to a boil. Heat a large skillet (frying pan) or wok over medium heat, then add the vegetable oil and sauté the pork belly, cut into pieces, until no longer pink. Add the sake and quickly stir. Add the cabbage, mushrooms, scallions, and carrot. Season with salt and pepper. Add the broth and sesame oil and simmer for 3 minutes.

4. Cook the noodles in the boiling water according to the package directions. Drain well. Divide the noodles among four medium bowls. Add the soup and serve.

This traditional noodle dish, which is served on Omisoka, or New Year's Eve, is said to enable you to overcome difficult past experiences. These long and thin noodles are easy to cut and they melt in the mouth.

[Midnight Diner]

Serves 4
Preparation time: 30 minutes
Cooking time: 20 minutes

Ingredients

- ½ cup (10 g) dried wakame seaweed
- 4 crab sticks
- 2 scallions (spring onions) or 4-inch (10-cm) length leek
- 12½ ounces (360 g) soba noodles*

For the broth
- 5 cups (1.2 liters) Dashi Broth (see page 9)
- ⅓ cup (90 ml) mirin
- ⅓ cup (90 ml) soy sauce
- ½ teaspoon salt

Toshikoshi Soba

1. Rehydrate the wakame in a bowl of cold water according to the package directions, then drain. Wash and slice the scallions into thin rings. Cut the crab sticks in half on the diagonal. Set aside.

2. To prepare the soba noodles, cook in a pot of boiling for a few minutes according to the package directions. They should be cooked to al dente, *kata me* in Japanese, because they will be reheated in boiling water before serving with a hot broth. Drain, rinse under cold water, and set aside.

3. To prepare the broth for the soba noodles, pour the dashi into a pot and add the mirin, soy sauce, and salt, then cook over medium heat for 2 minutes.

4. Bring a pot of water to a boil and reheat the cooked soba noodles. Drain and divide among four bowls. Reheat the broth and pour into the bowls. Garnish with the crab sticks, wakame, and scallion rings. Serve immediately.

* Soba is the name of noodles ranging in color from beige to dark gray-brown that are made from buckwheat flour, to which a greater or lesser amount of wheat flour has been added. Soba noodles are very nutritious.

This Japanese sandwich, which is especially popular among students, first appeared after World War II, but its fame has grown greatly since its appearance in numerous mangas.

[Midnight Diner]

Serves 4
Preparation time: 15 minutes
Cooking time: 5 minutes

Ingredients

- 1 tablespoon vegetable oil
- 2 knackwurst sausages or similar, thinly sliced on the diagonal
- ½ onion, peeled and thinly sliced
- 1 pointed cabbage leaf, julienned
- 2¼ cups (360 g) cooked yakisoba or ramen noodles
- ¼ cup (60 ml) yakisoba sauce*
- 4 hot dog buns

For serving
- Aonori seaweed flakes (optional)
- Beni shoga (red pickled ginger, optional)

Yakisoba Pan

1. Heat the oil in a large skillet (frying pan) or wok and sauté the sausages, onion, and cabbage. Add the noodles, followed by ¼ cup (60 ml) water. Using chopsticks, gently separate the noodles and cook for 2 minutes.
2. Pour the yakisoba sauce over the noodles. Stir and set aside.
3. Make a slit on the top of the buns.
4. Stuff the buns with cooked noodles. Sprinkle with aonori and add a little beni shoga to the middle of the bun. Serve immediately or cover with plastic wrap (clingfilm) and save for later.

* Yakisoba sauce is a sauce containing fruit and vegetables.

The Makanai:

Cooking for the Maiko House

Hirokazu Kore-eda — 2023

Adapted from a best-selling manga, this series is a delicately wrought tale of learning that is steeped in the treasures of Japanese gastronomy. Young Kiyo is fascinated by *maiko*—future *geiko*, or gei-shas—and goes to a traditional school in Kyoto to become one, but she fails in her attempt. However, when her inseparable friend Sumire pursues the same path with great success, Kiyo becomes the *makanai*, the cook who prepares the meals for her and her mentors, showing unwaver-ing enthusiasm and a genuine delight in tastes, dishes, and flavors. Serving them is an opportunity to interact with them on a daily basis, and for the viewer to discover our young protagonist's culinary talent and emblematic Japanese dishes—with all their rituals and secrets—in an elegant and poetic atmosphere. It is a sensitive homage to the culinary arts and fine foods of Japan. This book presents a selection of ten of these dishes, which are revealed in the course of the nine episodes that comprise the first season of the series.

Serves 4

Preparation time: 25 minutes

Cooking time: 15 minutes

Ingredients

- 11¼ ounces (320 g) dried somen noodles

For the dipping sauce
- ½ cup (125 ml) mentsuyu sauce*
- 1 cup (250 ml) ice water

For the garnishes
- 3 eggs
- 1 teaspoon superfine (caster) sugar
- 1 pinch salt
- 10 ounces (300 g) thinly sliced roast chicken (about 2 cups)
- ½ cucumber
- ½ bunch scallions (spring onions), green part only
- 1-inch (2.5-cm) piece fresh ginger
- 4 shiso (perilla) leaves
- Sesame seeds

* Sauce made with soy sauce, shiitake, dashi, and kombu

Cold Somen Noodles

1. To make the dipping sauce, mix the mentsuyu sauce with the ice water in a small bowl.
2. To prepare the garnish, beat the eggs in a bowl and season with a little sugar and salt. Pour into a hot nonstick skillet (frying pan) and turn to make a very thin omelet. Cut into thin strips.
3. Slice the cucumber into ¼-inch (7-mm)-thick rounds, then slice into julienne strips. Slice the scallions into thin rings and grate the ginger. Set aside in separate bowls.
4. Thinly slice the shiso leaves and place in a bowl. Put the sesame seeds into another small bowl. Arrange the cucumber, chicken, and omelet strips on a plate.
5. Bring a large pot of water to a boil. Add the noodles, spreading them around the pot like a fan. Cook according to the package directions, stirring from time to time with chopsticks, for about 2 minutes. Drain and rinse the noodles in a strainer under cold running water.
6. Divide the noodles into several portions and arrange in bunches on a serving dish or a few plates. Pour the dipping sauce into four bowls. To eat, dip the noodles in the sauce and mix with the different garnishes.

This simple soup deliciously highlights the sweetness and slight tartness of the tomatoes it contains.

[The Makanai: Cooking for the Maiko House]

Serves 4
Preparation time: 5 minutes
Cooking time: 10 minutes

Ingredients

- 10½ ounces (300 g) silken tofu
- 12 cherry tomatoes
- 2½ cups (600 ml) Dashi Broth (see page 9)
- 2 tablespoons miso paste

Tomato Miso Soup

1. Cut the tofu into ¾-inch (2-cm) squares. Wash the cherry tomatoes.
2. Add the dashi broth with the tomatoes and tofu to a pot, bring to a boil over medium heat, then remove from the heat.
3. Dissolve the miso paste in a ladle filled with the hot broth, then pour it into the pot.
4. Serve in individual bowls.

A traditional soup, the pretext in the episode of The Makanai, where it is prepared by the protagonist, is a delectable comparison of each of the residents of the school with one of its ingredients.

[The Makanai: Cooking for the Maiko House]

Serves 4
Preparation time: 20 minutes
Cooking time: 20 minutes

Ingredients

- 7 ounces (200 g) pork belly
- 1 onion
- 1 daikon (Japanese radish)
- 1 carrot
- 8¾ ounces (250 g) konjac (yam cake)
- ½ leek
- 10½ ounces (300 g) firm tofu
- ¼-inch (5-mm) piece ginger
- 2 scallions (spring onions)
- 1 tablespoon sesame oil
- 2½ cups (600 ml) Dashi Broth (see page 9)
- 2 tablespoons miso paste

Tonjiru
Pork and Vegetable Soup

1. Thinly slice the pork belly. Peel and halve the onion, then place the flat sides on the work surface and slice thinly. Peel and halve the daikon. Halve again lengthwise and cut into medium slices. Peel and halve the carrot lengthwise, then slice thinly. Cut the konjac into small rectangles. Bring water to a boil in a small saucepan. Add the konjac and cook for 2 to 3 minutes, then drain and set aside. Slice the leek diagonally. Cut the tofu into small cubes. Peel and mince (very finely chop) the ginger. Slice the scallions into thin rings and set aside in a bowl.

2. Place a casserole over medium heat. Add the oil. Sauté the pork belly for about 2 minutes, then add the onions and sauté. Add the daikon, carrot, konjac, leek, and ginger, then add just enough dashi broth to cover all the ingredients. Stir, bring to a boil, then reduce the heat. Skim the broth. Cover and simmer for about 15 minutes until the vegetables are cooked. Add the tofu pieces.

3. At the end, dissolve the miso paste in a ladle of broth and add it to the pot.

4. Serve in bowls, sprinkled with scallions.

映画の料理 Soups, Stews, and Noodles

Whisper of the Heart

Yoshifumi Kondo—1995

Fourteen-year-old Shizuku Tsukishima is a daydreamer and an avid reader who regularly visits the public library. One day she notices that every book she has borrowed had previously been checked out by a certain Seiji Amasawa, a coincidence that she finds intriguing. She later has several encounters with a young boy who makes fun of her a few times, a turn of events that marks the beginning of a friendship and a budding love interest. Based on the manga by Aoi Hiiragi, the screenplay for this animated feature film was written by Hayao Miyazaki, who was also fully involved in its production, giving it that unmistakable Studio Ghibli feel. He pays particular attention to the food eaten by the protagonists, as well as to the traditional crafts and artisans that are always featured in his work. A live-action sequel takes up the story ten years after the end of the animated movie; it was made in 2022 and released with the same name as the first, *Whisper of the Heart*.

////////////// **映画の料理** Soups, Stews, and Noodles

My Neighbor Totoro

Hayao Miyazaki—1988

Set in 1950s Japan, *My Neighbor Totoro* is a modern fairy tale, a hymn to nature, and an account of life's lessons all in one. It tells the story of young Mei and her older sister Satsuki, who move with their father into a new home in the country so that they can be closer to their mother, who is being treated at a particular hospital. There, closer to nature and to people, the two girls go on a journey of discovery that takes them to meet with and befriend the spirits of the forest, embodied by discreet creatures given the name Totoro, who are invisible to other humans. Where food is concerned, Satsuki prepares traditional bentos with sardines and umeboshi (Japanese pickled plums) for her father and sister as a picnic, and she works along with her sister to help their neighbor harvest vegetables in the fields. In this way, the movie also portrays Japanese food as an expression of the link between humans and nature.

Serves 4
Preparation time: 30 minutes
Cooking time: 20 minutes

Particularly popular in winter, this Japanese soup can include eggs, seafood, and chicken, similar to the one enjoyed by the sisters Shizuku and Shiro.

[Whisper of the Heart]

Ingredients

- 11¼ ounces (320 g) dried udon noodles
- 7 ounces (200 g) skinless, boneless chicken breast
- 7 cups (200 g) fresh spinach
- 5 cups (1.2 liters) Dashi Broth (see page 9)
- ⅓ cup (90 ml) mirin
- ⅓ cup (90 ml) soy sauce
- 2 large (150 g) carrots
- 4 shiitake or button mushrooms
- 2 scallions (spring onions)
- 4 eggs
- ½ teaspoon shichimi togarashi (Japanese seven spice mix)

Equipment
- Small cast iron or earthenware cooking pots

Nabeyaki Udon

1. Bring a large pot of water to a boil. Add the noodles, spreading them around the pot like a fan. Cook according to the package directions, stirring from time to time with chopsticks, for about 5 minutes. Drain and rinse the noodles in a colander under cold running water.

2. Thinly slice the chicken.

3. Wash the spinach and steam or microwave for 3 minutes. Rinse, dry, and coarsely chop. Set aside.

4. Bring the dashi broth to a boil. Remove from the heat and add the mirin and soy sauce. Set aside.

5. Peel and slice the carrots into thin strips. Wash and thinly slice the mushrooms. Slice the scallions into thin rings.

6. Divide the cooked udon noodles into four small earthenware pots. Add the carrots, chicken, mushrooms, and 1¼ cups (300 ml) dashi broth to each. Simmer over medium heat for about 10 minutes until the vegetables and meat are cooked.

7. When cooked, gather the noodles in each pot into a nest and crack 1 egg in the middle. Add the spinach. Cover the pots with their lids and let cook for 2 minutes. Remove from the heat and let stand for 2 minutes without lifting the lids. To finish, sprinkle the soup with scallions and shichimi togarashi and serve immediately.

Komatsuna, commonly known as Japanese mustard spinach, is a mild-flavored plant with thick leaves and stems.

[My Neighbor Totoro]

Serves 4
Preparation time: 5 minutes
Cooking time: 8 minutes

Ingredients

- 7 ounces (200 g) komatsuna
- 10½ ounces (300 g) silken tofu
- 2½ cups (600 ml) Dashi Broth (see page 9)
- 2 tablespoons miso paste

Miso Soup with Komatsuna

1. Cut the komatsuna* leaves into 1½-inch (4-cm) pieces.
2. Cut the tofu into ¾-inch (2-cm) squares.
3. Add the dashi broth with the komatsuna to a pot, bring to a boil over medium heat, and let simmer for about 3 minutes. Add the tofu, cook for 2 minutes, then remove from the heat.
4. Dissolve the miso paste in a ladle filled with the hot broth, then pour it into the pot.
5. Serve in individual bowls.

* Komatsuna is an Asian variety of oilseed rape. It is also known as Japanese mustard spinach. You can substitute with bok choy (pak choi), collard (spring) greens, or spinach.

Tampopo

Juzo Itami—1985

In a play on the famous spaghetti westerns, this is the world's first ramen western! The young widow Tampopo has been struggling to run a mediocre ramen restaurant in Tokyo on her own since the death of her husband. One day, a strange customer with the air of a cowboy, Goro, comes into her life. Mysterious, solitary, and with a fine palate, he tries to teach her the secrets of the culinary arts, taking her and his team of stooges on an adventure to concoct the ultimate ramen soup recipe. The movie brings together a series of parallel stories that share a common search for an ultimate recipe or the culinary grail. This comedy is often absurd, but it is always dynamic and unprecedented, filled with satire, and sends up different customs and genres. With its business dinners and eccentric, erotic, and culinary exploits, this movie has come to enjoy cult status. It is a joyful and out-of-the-ordinary movie that conveys an irresistible desire to discover all the subtleties of Japanese cuisine.

映画の料理 Soups, Stews, and Noodles

Ikiru

Akira Kurosawa—1952

Ikiru, "to live," is a masterpiece inspired by a novel by Tolstoy. It tells the story of Kanji Watanabe, the head of a government department who has become mute and paralyzed under the weight of routine and excessive bureaucracy. When he learns that he has an incurable cancer, he finally decides to give meaning to his life by making himself useful for the short time he has left to live and pushing for the realization of a project for local children that had been blocked until that time by the same bureaucracy to which he had contributed. Through the cleanup of an empty lot in the Hureocho neighborhood, the local children will finally have a decent playground, and this achievement will allow him to accept his death in peace. The movie paints the portrait of a man dealing with bureaucratic stagnation and breakdown of family life who discovers the joys of life, including the nightlife. This exceptional film is peppered with a gallery of colorful characters and several scenes featuring restaurant meals with traditional dishes. It is a reflection on the meaning of life and self-sacrifice.

Here is Japan's highly popular noodle soup that Tampopo, the eponymous protagonist of Juzo Itami's film, is striving to perfect.

[Tampopo]

Serves 4
Preparation time: 15 minutes
Cooking time: 10 minutes

Ingredients

- ½ sheet nori (dried seaweed)
- ⅕ leek
- 11¼ ounces (320 g) ramen noodles
- 12 slices roast pork
- ½ cup (80 g) menma (seasoned bamboo shoots, optional)

For the ramen broth
- 6¾ cups (1.6 liters) water
- 2 tablespoons instant ramen soup base
- ⅓ cup (80 ml) soy sauce
- 3 tablespoons cooking sake

Tampopo's Ramen
Noodle Soup

1. Cut the nori into rectangles. Thinly slice the leek.
2. Make the ramen broth. Heat the water in a large pot and add the instant soup base, soy sauce, and sake. At the same time, bring plenty of water to a boil in another pot for the noodles.
3. When the broth is hot, put the noodles into the pot of boiling water and cook for a few minutes until just tender but still firm to bite. Drain, divide among four bowls, and pour over the hot broth.
4. Add 3 slices roast pork to each bowl and garnish with sliced leek, bamboo shoots, and nori.

This tasty hot pot dish made with thinly sliced beef is also known as Japanese fondue.

[Ikiru]

Serves 4
Preparation time: 20 minutes
Cooking time: 10 minutes

Ingredients

- 1 leek
- 10½ ounces (300 g) firm tofu
- 1 bunch watercress
- 8¾ ounces (250 g) shirataki (konjac) noodles
- 8 shiitake or button mushrooms
- 1¼ pounds (600 g) beef (tenderloin/sirloin or round), thinly sliced as for carpaccio
- ½ teaspoon vegetable oil

For the sukiyaki sauce
- 2 tablespoons sugar
- scant ½ cup (100 ml) soy sauce
- scant ½ cup (100 ml) mirin
- scant ½ cup (100 ml) cooking sake

For serving
- 4 eggs

Equipment
- Cast iron cooking pot or skillet (frying pan)
- Tabletop burner or hot pot stove

Sukiyaki

Japanese Fondue

1. To make the sukiyaki sauce, mix the sugar with the soy sauce, mirin, and sake in a saucepan. Bring to a boil, stirring until the sugar has dissolved. Transfer the sauce to a container.

2. Slice the leek diagonally into ½-inch (1-cm) lengths. Cut the tofu into about ¾-inch (2-cm) cubes. Cut the watercress into 2-inch (5-cm) lengths.

3. Remove the mushroom stems (stalks) and cut a star pattern into the caps. Cut the shirataki noodles into 4-inch (10-cm) lengths, then blanch in a small saucepan of boiling water for about 2 minutes and drain.

4. Arrange the meat, mushrooms, leek, tofu, watercress, and noodles on a serving dish.

5. Heat a little oil in the pot on the tabletop burner. Quickly cook one-quarter of the beef slices (overcooking will make the meat tough and prevent it from hardening) and add a little sauce to the pot. Move the meat to one side and add one-quarter of the remaining ingredients to the other.

6. Break an egg into four small individual bowls and beat lightly.

7. Dip the beef and vegetables into the egg before eating. Cook the remaining ingredients in batches until used up, adding the sukiyaki sauce a little at a time.

What Did You Eat Yesterday

Naoko Ogigami—2006

This best-selling manga with millions of copies sold, multiaward-winning television series, and live-action movie released in 2021 tell the story of Kenji and Shiro, a gay couple living in Tokyo—one an affable and outgoing hairdresser, and the other a reserved and thrifty lawyer. This slice of life switches from their home life to their frustrations at work and are often comical. Many scenes depict the preparation of different meals by Shiro, a gourmet and excellent cook, from the purchasing of ingredients to sitting down to eat with his companion, a moment in which to share their daily experiences around the homemade dishes. Each episode of the television series is self-contained, with a detailed presentation of the recipe worthy of a cooking show. New episodes are forthcoming. The movie features a simple plot while retaining the essentials of the manga and series.

Made with only wheat flour, water, and salt, somen noodles cook very quickly, making this dish particularly easy.

[What Did You Eat Yesterday]

Serves 4
Preparation time: 20 minutes
Cooking time: 10 minutes

Ingredients

- 2 eggs
- ½-inch (1-cm) piece ginger
- 4 shiso (perilla) leaves (optional)
- 1 stalk celery
- ½ bunch cilantro (coriander)
- 8 scallions (spring onions) or 1 bunch chives
- ½ cucumber
- scant ½ cup (100 ml) water
- scant ½ cup (100 ml) mentsuyu sauce*
- 2 tomatoes
- 4 bundles somen noodles (about 10½ ounces/300 g)
- 7 ounces (200 g) canned tuna, drained
- 2 tablespoons toasted sesame seeds
- Vegetable oil
- Salt

* Sauce made with soy sauce, shiitake, dashi, and kombu

Somen

Noodle Salad with Aromatic Vegetables

1. To make scrambled eggs, break the eggs into a bowl, add 1 pinch of salt, and whisk briefly. Heat a little vegetable oil in a small nonstick skillet (frying pan) over medium heat. Add the beaten eggs, then stir and scrape the bottom of the skillet with a spatula. When the eggs are almost cooked, remove from the heat and stir to form small clumps. Let cool.

2. To prepare the vegetables, peel and thinly slice the ginger and the shiso leaves if using. Thinly slice the celery on the diagonal. Chop the cilantro. Slice the scallions into rings.

3. Slice the cucumber into ¼-inch (7-mm)-thick rounds, then slice into julienne strips. Mix the water with the mentsuyu sauce in a small bowl. Dice the tomatoes and mix with the sauce.

4. Cook the noodles in plenty of water. Then drain, rinse in cold water, and drain again. Divide among four plates. Pour the tomatoes and sauce over the noodles. Arrange the tuna in the middle and garnish with scrambled eggs, cucumber, and other vegetables. Sprinkle with the sesame seeds.

Serves 4
Preparation time: 30 minutes
Cooking time: 20 minutes
Resting time: 30 minutes

Yosenabe, which means "putting together in a pot," is a popular Japanese hot pot dish. The seafood and vegetables can be varied according to the season.

[What Did You Eat Yesterday]

Yosenabe

Surf and Turf Hot Pot

Ingredients

- 8-inch (20-cm) piece kombu (dried kelp)
- 3½ tablespoons (50 ml) mirin
- 3½ tablespoons (50 ml) soy sauce
- ½ napa (Chinese) cabbage (about 8¾ ounces/250 g)
- 1 carrot
- 1 leek
- 1 bunch watercress or spinach
- 10½ ounces (300 g) firm tofu
- 8 shiitake or button mushrooms
- 3½ ounces (100 g) shimeji mushrooms (optional)
- 8 clams
- 7 ounces (200 g) cod fillet
- 8 fresh pink shrimp (prawns)
- 8 scallops

Equipment
- Earthenware or cast iron cooking pot

1. Fill a pot with 4 cups (1 liter) water and add the kombu. Let soak for about 30 minutes, place over medium-low heat, and bring to almost boiling. Turn off the heat and remove the kombu. Add the mirin and soy sauce. Set aside.

2. Cut the cabbage leaves into 1½-inch (4-cm) lengths. Peel and cut the carrot and cut into julienne strips. Slice the leek diagonally into ½-inch (1-cm) lengths. Wash and chop the watercress. Cut the tofu into about ¾-inch (2-cm) cubes.

3. Remove the shiitake mushroom stems (stalks) and cut a star pattern into the caps. Cut off the base connecting the shimeji mushrooms and divide into small bunches. Rinse the clams under running water.

4. Cut the fish into 1¼ to 1½-inch (3–4 cm) cubes.

5. Cover the bottom of the pot with a layer of cabbage slices. Add all the vegetables to one side of the pot and place the fish and seafood on the other. Add the tofu. Cover and bring to a boil, then simmer for about 10 minutes.

6. Help yourself to the yosenabe directly from the pot, transferring it into individual bowls.

映画の料理

Fish and
Seafood

This is traditional, delicious, and hearty sushi dish is simple to make.

[The Asadas]

Ingredients

- 2¼ cups (450 g) Japanese short-grain (sushi) rice

For the sushi vinegar
- ⅓ cup (90 ml) rice vinegar or grain vinegar
- 2¼ tablespoons (30 g) superfine (caster) sugar
- 1½ teaspoons (10 g) salt

For the toppings
- 3 eggs
- 1 teaspoon superfine (caster) sugar
- 1 pinch salt
- 1½ cups (100 g) sugar snap peas
- 20 cooked shrimp
- 4 slices smoked salmon
- ⅓ cup (80 g) trout roe
- 4 sprigs chervil

Chirashizushi

1. To prepare the sushi vinegar, dissolve the salt and sugar in the vinegar in a small saucepan over low heat (without boiling, otherwise the acidity and flavor will be lost). Let cool.

2. Cook the rice (see page 11). While still hot, transfer to a large, previously moistened sushi rice tub or mixing bowl. Drizzle with the sushi vinegar and gently fold to combine without crushing the grains.

3. Cover the rice with a damp cloth and set aside.

4. To make the Japanese-style scrambled eggs, beat the eggs and season with a little sugar and salt. Pour into a nonstick skillet (frying pan) and cook over medium heat, stirring with 4 chopsticks (to separate into curds), as if cooking scrambled eggs. When almost cooked, remove from the heat and stir to form small clumps. Set aside.

5. Wash the peas, trim the ends, and cut in half on the diagonal. Place in a bowl with 1 tablespoon water in a heatproof bowl and cover with plastic wrap (clingfilm). Cook in the microwave for about 1 minute. Alternatively blanch in boiling water for 2 minutes. Drain and let cool.

6. Peel the shrimp, leaving on the tails. Cut a slit along the back and remove the black vein. Cut the smoked salmon into small pieces.

7. Divide the rice among four plates and top with scrambled egg. Add the shrimp, salmon, peas, and trout roe, then sprinkle with chervil leaves.

Serves 4
Preparation time: 10 minutes
Cooking time: 3 minutes
Resting time: 10 minutes

The famous technique known as tataki, or flash-searing, is typical of Japanese cuisine and ideal for cooking fish with delicate flesh, such as that of the particularly tender bonito.

[What Did You Eat Yesterday]

Ingredients

- 1 onion
- 2 cloves garlic
- ¼ bunch chives
- 4 bonito (skipjack tuna) steaks (1 pound 2 ounces/500 g)
- 2 tablespoons soy sauce
- 2 tablespoons toasted sesame oil
- Vegetable oil

Equipment
- Mandoline slicer

Bonito Tataki

1. Using the mandoline, finely slice the onion and garlic. Soak the onion in cold water for about 10 minutes, then drain. Set aside the garlic. Chop the chives.

2. Clean and pat dry the bonito steaks with (kitchen) paper towels. Heat a little vegetable oil in a nonstick skillet (frying pan) over very high heat. Sear the steaks for 30 seconds on each side. Transfer to a cutting (chopping) board and cut into slices about ¼ inch (7 mm) thick.

3. Arrange the bonito slices on plates. Top with the onion and garlic slices and sprinkle with the chives. Drizzle with the soy sauce and sesame oil.

Our Little Sister

Hirokazu Kore-eda—2015

Sachi, Yoshino, and Chika are sisters. At the funeral of their father, who had abandoned them fifteen years earlier, they meet their orphaned fourteen-year-old half-sister, Suzu, for the first time. They decide to invite her to live in their large family home. This is a sensitive homage to family, where tenderness and compassion are given pride of place, just like the fish dishes enjoyed by each of them separately in the Kamakura region, an original pretext for happy memories deployed in scenes that replace flashbacks and are scattered throughout the film. Although death is omnipresent, "I wanted to evoke it in a soothing way. Food is ideal for this, because it creates a bond between the living," the filmmaker explains. Simmered seafood, noodles and fresh fish, deep-fried mackerel or horse mackerel, dishes come and go, and the memories they leave behind resurface and are shared to the viewer's delight.

Mio's Cookbook

Haruki Kadokawa—2020

As foretold by a fortune-teller, inseparable best friends Mio and Noe are torn apart one tragic night in 1801 by the great Osaka flood, marking the end of their carefree childhood in the city. Now an orphan, Mio finds herself in Edo—as Tokyo was then called—where she explores and develops her incomparable culinary talents year after year, earning her fame as a chef and revisiting the flavors of her origins by adapting them to the times. News of her reputedly delicious dishes reaches Noe, who is now an *oiran*, a high-ranking courtesan, and reunited, food becomes the thread of a new-found friendship. Adapted from Kaoru Takada's series of ten historical novels, this movie is a visual treat with its reconstructions of the Edo period, the Yoshiwara pleasure district, and the meticulous preparation of culinary delights.

This tasty fish dish is a specialty of Umineko Shokudo, the family restaurant that the four sisters from Our Little Sister *frequently visit to share their memories.*

[Our Little Sister]

Serves 4
Preparation time: 20 minutes
Cooking time: 15 minutes

Ingredients

- 4 pointed cabbage leaves
- 8 horse mackerel fillets, cleaned
- 1 cup (125 g) all-purpose (plain) flour
- 1 egg
- 1 cup (80 g) panko bread crumbs
- 2 cups (500 ml) vegetable oil, for frying
- 8 cherry tomatoes
- Tonkatsu sauce* or soy sauce
- Salt and pepper

Equipment
- Cast iron Dutch oven, casserole or skillet (frying pan)

* A thick sauce made by simmering fruit and vegetables and seasoned with vinegar and spices

Deep-Fried Horse Mackerel

1. Thinly slice the cabbage and set aside.
2. Pat dry the fish fillets with (kitchen) paper towels. Season with salt and pepper.
3. Put the flour onto a plate. Break the egg into a bowl and beat with 2 tablespoons water. Put the bread crumbs onto another plate. Dredge the fish fillets in the flour, then dip in the egg and cover with bread crumbs.
4. Heat the oil in a cast iron Dutch oven, casserole, or skillet and, when hot, deep-fry the fillets for about 5 minutes until golden brown. Remove from the oil, shake off any excess, and let drain on a wire rack or paper towels.
5. On each of four plates, arrange a cabbage leaf, 2 horse mackerel fillets, and 2 cherry tomatoes. Serve with tonkatsu sauce or soy sauce.

This popular Japanese dish requires few ingredients and is very easy to prepare.

[The Wind Rises]

Serves 4
Preparation time: 10 minutes
Cooking time: 10 minutes

Ingredients

- ½-inch (1-cm) piece ginger
- 4 fresh mackerel fillets
- scant ½ cup (100 ml) water
- scant ½ cup (100 ml) cooking sake
- 1 tablespoon sugar
- ¼ cup (70 g) miso paste

Saba Misoni
Miso-Simmered Mackerel

1. Peel and chop the ginger.
2. Cut the mackerel fillets in half.
3. In a skillet (frying pan), combine the water and sake, add the sugar and ginger, and bring to a boil. Add the fish fillets, skin side up. When the liquid comes back to a boil, reduce the heat to medium. Cover and simmer fir about 5 minutes.
4. Put the miso paste into a small bowl, add 3 tablespoons cooking liquid, and stir to dissolve. Add the miso to the skillet. Reduce the heat and cook for an additional 5 minutes. Baste the mackerel with the cooking liquid from time to time.
5. Arrange the mackerel fillets on a plate and pour over a little cooking liquid.

映画の料理　Fish and Seafood

Samurai Gourmet

Masayuki Kusumi—2017

After years of hard work, sixty-year-old Takeshi has taken retirement. Unsure of what to do with the great deal of free time at his disposal, he realizes as he sips on a beer in the middle of the afternoon—an unusual luxury for him—that he has an entire world of eating and drinking to explore, in which he discovers and indulges a culinary passion buried deep inside. Accompanying him in this endeavor is his inner samurai, which he extravagantly and realistically unleashes in this twelve-part television series, enabling him to better enjoy what he really loves and to affirm his inner freedom. This hedonistic and endearing young retiree rediscovers a taste for flavor and simple pleasures as he gives in to the temptation of a delicious dish, where the preparation, plating, and enjoyment is experienced with great delight by Takeshi in each episode. This is a simple, soothing, and joyful series that entices in many different ways.

A classic of Japanese cuisine and raised to the status of a veritable culinary art, sashimi comprises slices of fresh fish or shellfish that are served raw.

[Samurai Gourmet]

Tuna Sashimi

Ingredients

- 2½-inch (6-cm) piece daikon (Japanese radish)
- 14 ounces (400 g) sashimi-grade tuna
- 4 shiso (perilla) leaves
- 1 tablespoon wasabi paste
- 4 tablespoons soy sauce

Equipment
- Mandoline slicer

1. Peel the daikon. Using the mandoline, slice it thinly lengthwise. Stack 4 or 5 slices on a cutting (chopping) board and cut into fine julienne strips. Repeat the process several times, then put the daikon strips into a bowl of very cold water.
2. Cut the tuna into 4 portions. Cut each portion into ½-inch (1-cm)-thick slices.
3. Drain the daikon and place a small amount on each plate. Add 1 shiso leaf to each plate. Arrange the tuna slices on the shiso leaf. Add a little wasabi to one side. Serve with soy sauce in ramekins.

映画の料理 Fish and Seafood

The Wind Rises

Hayao Miyazaki—2013

This animated film, directed by Hayao Miyazaki and loosely based on true events, depicts the life of Jiro, an ingenious aeronautical engineer who designed bombers that were used in World War II. It is set against a historical backdrop spanning his youth in 1918 to Japan's entry into the war, including the Great Kanto Earthquake and Great Depression.

Although he soon realized that his poor eyesight would hinder him from becoming a pilot, Jiro still dreamed of flying, and after showing his brilliance while studying at Tokyo Imperial University, he joined a major aeronautical company in 1927, where his exceptional talent soon became apparent. Through his love of Nahoko and his friendship with his colleague, Honjo, Miyazaki re-creates this extraordinary inventor's journey to war inspired by a quote from Paul Valéry: "Le vent se lève … il faut tenter de vivre" ("The wind is rising … we must try to live"), which is highly symbolic of the protagonists' destiny. The film is a wonder of animation with multiple messages about the human soul, creativity, and its downsides, in the tradition of Studio Ghibli's masterful and beautifully crafted realism.

*Sometimes called makimono, and often sim-
ply known as maki or sushi rolls, makizushi
is one of the most recognizable Japanese
culinary creations.*

[Mio's Cookbook]

Ingredients

- 1½ cups (300 g) Japanese short-grain (sushi) rice
- 8¾ ounces (250 g) canned solid tuna in oil
- ½ cucumber
- 4 sheets nori (dried seaweed)
- Wasabi paste
- Soy sauce

For the sushi vinegar
- ¼ cup (60 ml) rice vinegar or grain vinegar
- 1½ tablespoons (20 g) superfine (caster) sugar
- 1 teaspoon salt

Equipment
- 1 *makisu* (sushi) mat

Tuna and Cucumber Makizushi

1. To prepare the sushi vinegar, dissolve the salt and sugar in the vinegar in a small saucepan over low heat (without boiling, otherwise the acidity and flavor will be lost). Let cool.
2. Cook the rice (see page 11). While still hot, transfer to a large, previously moistened sushi rice tub or mixing bowl. Drizzle with the sushi vinegar and gently fold to combine without crushing the grains.
3. Prepare the garnish. Peel and cut the cucumber into quarters lengthwise, then cut quarters in half widthwise. Drain, crumble, and mix the tuna with 1 teaspoon soy sauce in a small bowl.
4. Cut the nori sheets in half horizontally. Lay a nori half-sheet on the mat. Wet your hands and spread one-eighth of the rice over a nori sheet to a thickness of about ½ inch (1 cm). Place one-eighth of the tuna and a cucumber stick on the bottom third of the nori. Roll the mat from bottom to top, holding the ingredients in place with your fingertips. Press the maki firmly several times across its entire width while rolling. Repeat the process until all the ingredients are used.
5. Place the roll on a cutting (chopping) board. Wet the blade of a sharp knife in water and slice the roll into five or six pieces. Serve accompanied with soy sauce and wasabi.

Serves 4
Preparation time: 15 minutes
Cooking time: 20 minutes
Resting time: 5 minutes

This traditional Japanese dish, a savory egg custard, is served cold or warm, typically as an appetizer.

[Mio's Cookbook]

Ingredients

- 4 cooked shrimp (prawns)
- 4 shiitake or button mushrooms
- 8 chives
- Organic orange or yuzu zest

**For the custard
and dashi broth**
- 3 eggs
- 2⅓ cups (550 ml) Dashi Broth (see page 9)
- 1 teaspoon soy sauce
- 1 teaspoon mirin
- 1 teaspoon salt

Torotoro Chawanmushi

Savory Egg Custard with Shrimp and Shiitake Mushrooms

1. If using instant dashi granules, dissolve with 1 tablespoon hot water in a bowl, then add 2⅓ cups (550 ml) water. Add the soy sauce, mirin, and salt. Break the eggs into a separate bowl and beat with a whisk. Strain the eggs into the dashi through a conical strainer (sieve).

2. Remove the stems (stalks) from the mushrooms and slice thinly. Peel the shrimp, leaving on the tails. Cut a slit along the back and remove the black vein.

3. Divide the mushrooms and shrimp among small bowls. Cover the ingredients with the custard mixture and cover each bowl with aluminum foil.

4. Make a bain-marie by filling a large pot to two-thirds of the height of the bowls with water, then place the bowls in it. Cover and bring to a boil over medium heat. Cook for 3 minutes, then reduce heat to low and cook for an additional 10 minutes. Remove from the heat and let stand, covered, for 5 minutes. Take the bowls out of the pot, remove the foil, and garnish with a little organic orange zest and chopped chives.

映画の料理

Meat and
Eggs

Serves 4
Preparation time: 5 minutes
Cooking time: 5 minutes

Ingredients

- 1 eggplant
- 1 green bell pepper
- ½-inch (1-cm) piece ginger
- 7 ounces (200 g) pork belly
- 2 tablespoons vegetable oil
- 1 tablespoon sesame oil

For the miso and mustard sauce
- 2 tablespoons miso paste
- ½ cup (120 ml) water
- 2 teaspoon soy sauce
- 2 tablespoon sugar
- 1 teaspoon karashi (Japanese mustard) or regular mustard

Equipment
- Wok or skillet (frying pan)

Pork and Eggplant Stir-Fry

1. To make the miso and mustard sauce, mix all the sauce ingredients in a bowl until combined.
2. Halve the eggplant lengthwise. Place the flat sides on the work surface and cut into ½-inch (1-cm)-thick slices, then halve each slice again. Halve the bell peppers lengthwise, then slice the same way as the eggplant. Peel and mince (very finely chop) the ginger.
3. Thinly slice the pork.
4. Heat the oil in a wok over high heat. Sauté the pork pieces for about 2 minutes, then add the bell pepper, eggplant, and ginger. When all the ingredients are cooked, add the miso and mustard sauce. Cook for a few additional minutes, stirring constantly, then drizzle with the sesame oil.
5. Serve in a dish accompanied with a bowl of steamed rice (see page 11), miso soup (see pages 49 and 59), and pickled cucumber.

This easy-to-prepare, protein-rich dish is the first devised by Kiyo, the protagonist of The Makanai, *when she finds herself in charge of the kitchen.*

[The Makanai: Cooking for the Maiko House]

Serves 4
Preparation time: 15 minutes
Cooking time: 10 minutes

Ingredients

- 2⅓ cups (450 g) Japanese short-grain (sushi) rice
- ⅕ bunch chives
- 1 onion
- 10½ ounces (300 g) skinless, boneless chicken breast
- 1 cup (250 ml) Dashi Broth (see page 9)
- 3½ tablespoons (50 ml) soy sauce
- 2 tablespoons superfine (caster) sugar
- ⅓ cup (80 ml) mirin
- 8 eggs
- Ichimi togarashi (Japanese red chili flakes) or Espelette pepper

Oyakodon
Chicken and Egg Rice Bowl

1. Cook the rice (see page 11). Wash and chop the chives. Set aside.
2. Peel and halve the onion. Cut each onion half into slices about ¼ inch (5 mm) thick. Cut the chicken breasts into 1¼-inch (3-cm) cubes.
3. Put the dashi broth into a large skillet (frying pan) and add the soy sauce, sugar, and mirin. Bring to a boil over medium heat. Add the chicken and onion and cook for 5 minutes.
4. Break the eggs into a bowl and beat briefly. Add the eggs to the skillet, cover, and cook over medium heat for 1 to 2 minutes. Remove the skillet from the heat, keep covered, and set aside for 1 to 3 minutes, depending on how cooked you prefer the egg.
5. Divide the egg and chicken mixture into four portions. Fill four large bowls with rice and top with a portion of chicken and egg. Garnish with a little chopped chives. Serve accompanied with chili flakes.

Serves 4
Preparation time: 15 minutes
Cooking time: 10 minutes
Resting time: 10 minutes

This is the special, traditional Japanese sandwich made by Kiyo, the protagonist of The Makanai, *for her friend Sumire on the day she becomes a* maiko.

[The Makanai: Cooking for the Maiko House]

Ingredients

- 6 eggs
- ¼ cup (55 g) mayonnaise
- 2 tablespoons milk
- 8 slices sandwich bread
- 2 tablespoons (25 g) butter
- Salt and freshly ground white pepper

Tamago Sando

Japanese Egg Sandwich

1. To make the hard-boiled eggs, use a ladle to immerse the eggs into a pot of boiling water and cook for 10 minutes. Transfer to cold water to stop the cooking process and then peel.
2. Halve the hard-boiled eggs. In a bowl, mash the yolks with a fork while gradually adding the mayonnaise and milk. Finely dice the egg whites and combine. Season with salt and pepper.
3. Spread butter on one side of each of the bread slices, then spread the egg mixture over the buttered side of four slices. Cover with the four remaining slices.
4. Place one sandwich on top of another, cover each stack with an upturned plate, and let stand for 10 minutes.
5. Cut the crusts off the bread, then cut each sandwich into 12 pieces (cut each sandwich in four strips, then cut each strip into thirds).

Serves 4
Preparation time: 20 minutes
Cooking time: 20 minutes
Resting time: 30 minutes

These famous skewers of bite-size pieces are typically cooked on a grill, like at the restaurant where Takeshi, protagonist of the Samurai Gourmet series, goes on his own one night.

[Samurai Gourmet]

Ingredients

- 4 chicken livers
- 2 skinless, boneless chicken breasts
- 8 scallions (spring onions), green parts only
- 1 onion
- 4 shiitake or button mushrooms

For the dipping sauce
- 2 tablespoons superfine (caster) sugar
- scant ½ cup (100 ml) soy sauce
- ⅓ cup (80 ml) mirin
- ⅓ cup (80 ml) cooking sake

Yakitori

Chicken Skewers

1. To make the sauce, mix the sugar with the soy sauce, mirin, and sake in a saucepan. Bring to a boil and cook over high heat until the sauce is reduced by half and syrupy. Transfer the hot sauce to a small bowl.

2. Soak 12 bamboo skewers in cold water for 30 minutes to keep them from burning. Cut the chicken breasts into uniform 1 to 1¼-inch (2–3 cm) cubes. Cut each chicken liver into 4 uniform pieces. Wash and cut the scallions into 1¼-inch (3-cm) pieces.

3. Prepare four skewers by threading each with 4 liver pieces, alternating with 2 scallion pieces. Prepare eight more skewers by threading each with 3 cubes of chicken breast, alternating with 2 scallion pieces. Optionally, you can prepare two more skewers be threading with white onion (peeled and cut into ⅝-inch/1.5-cm thick rounds) and two more with mushrooms (cut into ⅝-inch/1.5 cm thick slices).

4. Place the skewers in a shallow dish and brush on all sides with the sauce. Arrange the skewers on a broiler (grill) rack set over a drip tray. Broil (grill) the skewers for a few minutes, regularly turning and brushing them with the sauce.

映画の料理 Meat and Eggs

Hold Me Back

Akiko Oku—2020

Mitsuko, at the age of thirty-one, is a solitary person. Living in a bubble of her making, she finds it hard to adapt to social relations and is unhappy at work. She finds herself in much better company with her inner voice, an alter-ego she calls A, and whom she consults assiduously. The happily single Mitsuko enthusiastically pursues her passion of cooking and perfecting her recipes in her small apartment in Tokyo. That is until love comes calling in the form of a young salesman named Tada. This romantic comedy, based on a novel by Risa Wataya, is brought to life by a sensitive, fragile, and radiant actress. Among other things, the director tackles the theme of singlehood and loneliness in Japan, with its paradoxes. Between social pressure and the doubts or fears of wanting to change her life, Mitsuko wonders what would happen if she were to start a real relationship for good. Would her precious little inner advisor disappear?

This Japanese beef and potato stew is a good example of traditional family cooking.

[Hold Me Back]

Serves 4
Preparation time: 15 minutes
Cooking time: 20 minutes

Ingredients

- 4 medium potatoes (about 14 ounces/400 g)
- 2 carrots
- 2 onions
- 7 ounces (200 g) beef (a tender cut, such as tenderloin/sirloin)
- 2 tablespoons vegetable oil
- 2½ cups (600 ml) water
- 1 cup (100 g) green beans

Seasoning*
- ¼ teaspoon instant dashi granules
- 1 tablespoon superfine (caster) sugar
- 1 tablespoon cooking sake
- 1 tablespoon mirin
- 3 tablespoons soy sauce

* Substitute teriyaki sauce for all the seasoning ingredients.

Niku Jyaga
Potato and Beef Stew

1. Peel, wash, and cut the potatoes and carrots into chunks. Peel and halve the onions. Cut the onion halves into ¼-inch (5-mm)-thick slices. Also cut the meat into ¼-inch (5-mm)-thick pieces.

2. Heat the oil in a casserole and brown the meat and onion over very high heat for 3 minutes. Add the potatoes, carrots, and water and bring to a boil. Skim and let cook, about 3 minutes.

3. Reduce the heat, then add the dashi granules, sugar, sake, mirin, and soy sauce. Mix to combine.

4. Cover and cook for 15 minutes, then add the green beans and let cook for an additional 5 minutes. Divide the meat, vegetables, and broth among four bowls.

Tokyo Story

Yasujiro Ozu—1953

This movie is considered an absolute master-piece of motion picture history by cinephiles around the world. However, it was only released in France in the late 1970s, finally introducing Ozu, its director, to that country. It tells the story of a retired couple who have left their country home to visit their children in Tokyo. It becomes obvious how little time and space their children have in their busy lives to devote to them. Only their widowed daughter-in-law, Noriko, the wife of their son who died in the war, welcomes their presence and gives them the time and attention they had expected from their own children. The movie portrays the inexorable decline of the traditional Japanese family system in the postwar period, for which Ozu's unique aesthetic use of a static camera is very effective. This film is filled with emotions; life lessons on old age, estrangement, and loneliness; moments of humor and bitterness; and a calm that is both fascinating and moving.

An Autumn Afternoon

Yasujiro Ozu—1962

Shuhei is a widower living with his youngest son and his daughter Michiko, who is of marriageable age but is devoted to him and reassuringly staves off loneliness. One evening, over a glass of sake, one of his friends suggests a possible match for his daughter, leading Shuhei to realize that he will have to free her from his hold, even if his fear of being alone and his selfishness make him reject the prospect. The example of one of his former teachers, now fallen on hard times and whose daughter has sacrificed her youth to take care of him, makes him reconsider his vision of things. This movie, the last by the great director Ozu, is a magnificent comparison between the traditional and patriarchal Japan and postwar Japan, between the simple joys and the melancholy of the older generation. Much of its unique charm comes from its minimalism and particular aesthetics. The original title of this film, *Sanma no aji*, "The Taste of Sanma," refers to a popular Japanese fish that is typically eaten in fall.

The name of this iconic Japanese dish is a contraction of tonkatsu, *breaded pork cutlets, and* donburi, *rice bowl dish, which is exactly what it is.*

[Tokyo Story]

Serves 4
Preparation time: 15 minutes
Cooking time: 5 minutes

Ingredients

- 2⅓ cups (450 g) Japanese short-grained (sushi) rice
- ⅕ bunch chives
- 1 onion
- 4 freshly cooked tonkatsu (breaded pork cutlets, see page 113)
- 4 eggs
- Ichimi togarashi (Japanese red chili flakes) or Espelette pepper

For the katsudon
- 1¼ cups (300 ml) Dashi Broth (see page 9)
- scant ⅓ cup (70 ml) soy sauce
- scant ⅓ cup (70 ml) mirin
- 2 tablespoons superfine (caster) sugar

Katsudon

Pork Cutlet and Egg Rice Bowl

1. Cook the rice (see page 11). Wash and chop the chives. Set aside.

2. Peel and halve the onion. Cut each onion half to slices about ¼ inch (5 mm) thick. Cut each tonkatsu into 8 strips.

3. To prepare the katsudon, combine the dashi broth, soy sauce, mirin, and sugar in a bowl. To each of two medium skillets (frying pans), add half of the dashi mixture and bring to a boil over medium heat, then add half of the onions. Cook for 3 minutes. Add 16 strips of tonkatsu to each skillet.

4. Break the eggs into a bowl and beat briefly. Add half the beaten eggs to each skillet, cover, and cook over medium heat for 1 to 2 minutes. Remove the skillets from the heat, keep covered, and set aside for 1 to 3 minutes, depending on how cooked you prefer the egg.

5. Fill four large bowls with rice. Divide the tonkatsu omelets into four portions and arrange one portion on top of the rice in each bowl. Add the freshly cooked sliced breaded pork cutlets and garnish with the chopped chives. Serve accompanied with chili flakes.

A typical Japanese dish, these pork cutlets encrusted in panko bread crumbs are simple to make and delicious.

[An Autumn Afternoon]

Serves 4
Preparation time: 15 minutes
Cooking time: 20 minutes

Ingredients

- 4 pointed cabbage leaves
- 1 lemon
- 4 (¾-inch/2-cm-thick) slices boneless pork loins or pork chops
- 1 cup (125 g) all-purpose (plain) flour
- 1 egg
- 2 tablespoons water
- 1 cup (80 g) panko bread crumbs
- 2 cups (500 ml) vegetable oil, for frying
- Tonkatsu sauce* or soy sauce
- Salt and pepper

Equipment
- Cast iron Dutch oven, casserole or skillet (frying pan)

* A thick sauce made by simmering fruit and vegetables and seasoned with vinegar and spices

Tonkatsu
Breaded Pork Cutlets

1. Thinly slice the cabbage and set aside. Cut the lemon into 8 wedges.
2. Season the pork with salt and pepper.
3. Put the flour onto a plate. Break the egg into a bowl and beat with the water. Put the bread crumbs onto another plate. Dredge the pork cutlets in the flour, then dip in the egg and cover with bread crumbs.
4. Put the oil into the Dutch oven, casserole or skillet and deep-fry the cutlets for about 5 minutes on each side, until golden brown. Remove from the oil, shake off any excess, and let drain on a rack or (kitchen) paper towels.
5. Cut the cutlets into slices, then make a bed of cabbage on each plate, top with the sliced cutlets, and add the lemon wedges. Serve with tonkatsu sauce or soy sauce.

映画の料理 Meat and Eggs

Midnight Diner

Shinya Shokudo

Various directors,
first episode broadcast in 2009

The owner of a late-night *izakaya*—the Japanese version of a diner—in Tokyo's Shinjuku district and his clientele are the subject of this television series, originally adapted from a manga. Although "Master"—as the reserved, calm, and well-informed owner and chef is called by his customers—limits his menu to a single dish, tonjiru, a pork and miso soup, he is nevertheless willing to cook anything his customers ask for, provided he has the necessary ingredients. From midnight to seven o'clock in the morning, a stream of solitary customers as varied as a yakuza, a newspaper delivery boy, or a stripper, come to him for a late-night meal. With each episode featuring one particular customer, his or her personal connection to a specific dish, and a subject or even a conflict to be resolved, this is an original, sensitive, and often philosophical way of showcasing more than one Japanese specialty that goes beyond any social or cultural barriers. There is a bonus feature at the end of each episode in which the Master explains how to make the featured dish.

The flavor of this soup can be varied depending on the spices used.

[Midnight Diner: Tokyo Stories]

Serves 1
Preparation time: 15 minutes
Cooking time: 10 minutes

Hot Pot for One

Ingredients

- Shichimi togarashi (Japanese seven spice mix) or Espelette pepper

For the soup
- 2 napa (chinese) cabbage leaves
- 1¾ ounces (50 g) enoki mushrooms
- 1¾ ounces (50 g) medium-firm tofu (momen-dofu)
- 4 slices pork belly
- 1¾ cups (400 ml) Dashi Broth (see page 9)
- 2 tablespoons cooking sake

For the ponzu sauce
- 2 tablespoons teriyaki sauce
- 2 tablespoons orange juice
- 1 teaspoon rice vinegar

Equipment
- Earthenware or cast iron cooking pot

1. Cut the cabbage leaves into small pieces. Cut off the root end of the mushroom stems (stalks) and discard. Divide the mushrooms into small bunches. Cut the tofu into ¾-inch (2-cm)-thick pieces, then into about 1½-inch (4-cm) squares. Cut the pork belly slices into 2 or 3 pieces.

2. Make an orderly arrangement with these ingredients in the pot. Add the dashi broth and sake. Cover and simmer for 5 minutes. Skim and cook for an additional 5 minutes. Mix together the ingredients for the ponzu sauce and transfer to a small bowl for serving. Season the soup with shichimi togarashi. To enjoy, dip the different ingredients into the ponzu sauce.

This is a simple dish, but it takes practice to roll and fold the omelet successfully. A rectangular omelet pan is also an absolute must!

[Midnight Diner: Tokyo Stories]

Serves 1
Preparation time: 3 minutes
Cooking time: 5 minutes

Ingredients

- 3 extra-large (UK large) eggs
- 1½ teaspoons sugar
- ½ teaspoon soy sauce
- Vegetable oil

Equipment
- Nonstick rectangular omelet pan

Tamagoyaki
Japanese Omelet

1. Break the eggs into a bowl and whisk. Add the sugar and soy sauce and mix until combined.

2. Heat the pan over medium heat. Using chopsticks, dip a folded (kitchen) paper towel in the oil and coat the inside of the pan with a thin layer. Pour a thin layer of the egg mixture. When the thin omelet is almost cooked, fold about 1¼ inches (3 cm) of each of the long edges toward the center with a spatula and fold over a second time, then roll it tightly to one side of the pan. Apply more oil to the empty part of the pan and pour a thin layer of the egg mixture. Let cook and repeat the rolling process. Serve on a plate.

映画の料理

Rice and
Vegetables

Agebitashi, *a typically Japanese summer
dish of deep-fried eggplant soaked in a light
broth, is a treat for the taste buds.*

[The Makanai: Cooking for the Maiko House]

Serves 4
Preparation time: 20 minutes
Cooking time: 15 minutes

Ingredients

- ½ daikon (Japanese radish)
- 2 scallions (spring onions)
- ½-inch (1-cm) piece of ginger
- 2 medium eggplants
  (aubergines)
- 2 cups (500 ml) vegetable oil,
  for frying
- ¾ cup (10 g) katsuobushi
  (dried bonito flakes)

For the broth
- ½ cup (125 ml) Dashi Broth
  (see page 9)
- 3 tablespoons mirin
- 3 tablespoons cooking sake*
- 3 tablespoons soy sauce*
- 1 tablespoon superfine (caster)
  sugar

* You can substitute ⅓ cup (75 ml)
teriyaki sauce for the soy sauce
and sake.

Agebitashi
Deep-Fried Eggplant Soaked in a Light Broth

1. In a small saucepan, combine all the broth ingredients,
   bring to a boil, and remove from heat (cover to prevent
   evaporation).
2. Peel and grate the daikon. Slice the scallions into thin rings.
   Peel and grate the ginger.
3. Prepare the eggplant. Cut off and discard the tops and
   halve lengthwise. Score the skin side with diagonal inci-
   sions spaced ¼ inch (5 mm) apart. Cut each half into 3 or
   4 sections.
4. Heat the frying oil to 340°F (170°C). Check the temperature
   by dipping chopsticks into it: medium champagne-like
   bubbles should appear at this temperature.
5. Place a few eggplant pieces in the oil, skin side down. Let fry
   for about 2 minutes. Remove, shake off the excess oil, and
   let drain on a wire rack or (kitchen) paper towels. Repeat the
   process with the remaining eggplant.
6. Transfer the eggplant to a bowl. Heat the broth and pour
   over the eggplant.
7. Arrange the soaked eggplant in a serving dish and set aside
   the broth. Sprinkle with katsuobushi and top with grated daikon and ginger. Pour over 1 tablespoon broth and garnish
   with scallion rings.

A super-quick recipe with a stunning result: tender eggplant with the sweet-and-sour flavors of a miso sauce.

[Midnight Diner]

Serves 4
Preparation time: 5 minutes
Cooking time: 20 minutes

Ingredients

- 4 small eggplants (aubergines)

For the miso sauce
- scant ⅓ cup (80 g) red (aka) miso paste
- 3 tablespoons hazelnut butter or tahini
- 2 tablespoons maple syrup or sugar
- 3 tablespoons mirin or apple juice

Eggplant with Miso

1. Make the miso sauce. Put the miso paste into a small saucepan and add the hazelnut butter, maple syrup, and mirin. Place over medium heat and bring to almost boiling, stirring constantly, then remove from the heat. Set aside.

2. Roast the eggplant in the oven at 400°F (200°C/Gas Mark 6) for about 20 minutes. When cooked, cut an incision down the middle. Coat the inside of each eggplant with the miso sauce.

Serves 4
Preparation time: 30 minutes
Resting time: 10 minutes
Cooking time: 35 minutes

The essential Japanese all-in-one meal is balanced and ready to enjoy, and it comes with a variety of dishes and accompaniments to suit every taste!

[Little Forest]

Bento

Onigiri with Miso, Omelet, Radish

Ingredients

- 8 shiso (perilla) leaves
- 4 bamboo leaves (optional) or a bento box
- Tamagoyaki (rolled omelet, see page 119)

For the onigiri (rice balls), makes 8
- 2⅔ cups (450 g) Japanese short-grain (sushi) rice

For the miso glaze
- scant ⅓ cup 80 g red (aka) miso paste
- 3 tablespoons tahini
- 2 tablespoons maple syrup or sugar
- 3 tablespoons mirin or apple juice

For the *tsukemono* (Japanese pickles)
- 2-inch (5-cm) piece kombu (dried kelp)
- 1 bunch radishes
- 1 teaspoon salt
- ½ teaspoon superfine (caster) sugar
- 1 teaspoon grated organic orange zest

1. Cook the rice (see page 11).
2. To prepare the *tsukemono*, place the kombu on a plate, moisten with 2 tablespoons water, and let soak for 10 minutes. Wash the radishes and put into a resealable freezer bag along with the salt, sugar, and orange zest. Using scissors, cut the kombu into thin strips and add to the bag with the soaking water. Seal the bag and gently massage. Set aside.
3. To make the miso glaze, combine all the ingredients in a small saucepan. Place over medium heat and bring to almost boiling, stirring constantly with a whisk, then remove from the heat. The sauce should be creamy. Transfer to a container and cover with plastic wrap (clingfilm). Set aside.
4. Make the omelet (see page 119). Slice it into eighths.
5. To make the triangle onigiri, use the rice while still hot. Lay a square of plastic wrap on a cutting (chopping) board. Place one-eighth of the rice in the middle, spreading with a spoon, then draw all the sides of the plastic wrap together and twist the top to seal. Using your hands, press each side to form the rice into a triangle shape. Peel off the plastic wrap. Lightly season with salt. Repeat the operation to make the remaining seven onigiri. To finish, coat the top of each onigiri with the miso glaze. Cook in the oven until the miso glaze turns golden. Remove from the oven and top each onigiri with a shiso leaf.
6. Assemble the bento by arranging 2 onigiri, 2 tamago yaki pieces, and a few pickled radishes on each bamboo leaf and wrap.

Serves 4
Preparation time: 20 minutes
Cooking time: 15 minutes
Resting time: Overnight + 1 hour

The particular feature of this dish is that all the ingredients are cooked together with the rice. In fact, takikomi gohan *means "rice cooked with."*

[What Did You Eat Yesterday]

Takikomi Gohan

Japanese Mixed Rice

Ingredients

- 2 (4-ounce/115-g) salmon fillet portions, any skin and bones removed
- 2⅓ cups (450 g) Japanese short-grain (sushi) rice
- 1 carrot
- 5¼ ounces (150 g) maitake or shiitake mushrooms
- 3½ ounces (100 g) Jerusalem artichokes (⅔ cup prepared)
- 2 cups (500 ml) water

For the salmon salt solution (brine)
- scant 1 cup (200 ml) water
- 2 tablespoons fine salt
- 1 tablespoon sugar

For the seasoning
- 3 tablespoons soy sauce
- 3 tablespoons cooking sake
- 4-inch (10-cm) piece kombu (dried kelp)
- 1 teaspoon sesame oil

1. Halve the salmon fillets lengthwise and place in a plastic bag. Add the salt, sugar, and water and marinate overnight in this salt solution.

2. To prepare the rice, wash the rice in a bowl under cold running water, stir with your hand, then quickly discard the water. Repeat the operation until the water turns completely clear. Let stand about 1 hour until the rice turns white (it will be translucent at first). Soak the kombu in 2 cups (500 ml) water.

3. Peel and slice the carrot into strips. Cut the base off the mushrooms, then cut into small pieces. Scrub the Jerusalem artichokes to remove any impurities. Cut into rounds about ¼ inch (5 mm) thick, soak in water, and drain.

4. Drain the rice and salmon. In a pot, combine the rice with the kombu soaking water, all the seasoning ingredients (including the kombu), salmon, and vegetables. Cover, place over high heat, bring to a boil, and let cook for about 3 minutes. Reduce the heat to low and let simmer for 10 minutes. Remove from the heat and let stand for 15 minutes with the lid on to let the rice finish steaming. Divide among bowls.

Serves 4
Preparation time: 5 minutes
Cooking time: 15 minutes
Resting time: 30 minutes

Seemingly simple, this warm and nourishing dish takes full advantage of the fine texture of the tofu.

[The Makanai: Cooking for the Maiko House]

Ingredients

- 2 (14-ounce/400-g) blocks medium-firm tofu (momen-dofu) or silken tofu
- 1 bunch watercress
- 4-inch (10-cm) piece kombu (dried kelp)
- 1 tablespoon cooking sake
- 1 pinch salt

For the sauce*
- ½ cup (125 ml) soy sauce
- 2 tablespoons cooking sake
- 2 tablespoons mirin
- ½ cup (6 g) katsuobushi (dried bonito flakes)

Extras (optional)
- 1 scallion (spring onion), green part only
- Grated ginger
- Shichimi togarashi (Japanese seven spice mix)
- Yuzu kosho (green yuzu and chili paste)

Equipment
- Earthenware or cast iron cooking pot

* You can substitute teriyaki sauce for the sauce ingredients.

Yudofu
Boiled Tofu with Sauce and Spices

1. To make a kombu dashi broth, soak the kombu in about 3⅓ cups (800 ml) water for 30 minutes in a pot. To speed up the process, place the pot over very low heat until hot (without boiling).

2. To make the sauce, combine all the ingredients, except the katsuobushi, in a small saucepan and bring to a boil, then add the katsuobushi. Stir with chopsticks and let cook for 1 to 2 minutes. Without straining, transfer the sauce to a small bowl.

3. Cut each tofu block into 6 cubes. Wash and coarsely chop the watercress. Bring the kombu dashi broth to a boil, add the sake and pinch of salt, then add the tofu pieces. After a few minutes, when the tofu is hot, add the watercress and other ingredients of your choice. Serve the tofu in four bowls and drizzle with the sauce.

映画の料理 Rice and Vegetables

The Asadas

Ryota Nakano—2020

Based on a true story, this movie portrays the life of Masashi Asada, a passionate professional photographer, from his beginnings to his finding fame in the wake of the 2011 tsunami, when he went in search of the missing. His has one subject, his family. He immortalizes them in 1,001 situations, poses, and costumes that reflect an ideal, dreamed-of life that is far removed from their daily routine: as employees at a ramen restaurant, firefighters, race car drivers, and members of a rock band, among others.

Unwavering optimism, shared joy, solidarity, and the unsuspected virtues of photography shine throughout this film, which balances humor and emotion from start to finish, and in which Japanese food contributes to the warm, authentic feeling it gives, as when the father of the family prepares tasty dishes for his beloved clan.

Every curry rice contains its own secret ingredient to make it truly personal. Grated apple adds a special touch in this recipe.

[The Asadas]

Serves 4
Preparation time: 15 minutes
Cooking time: 30 minutes

Ingredients

- 2⅓ cups (450 g) Japanese short-grain (sushi) rice
- 2 carrots
- 2 medium potatoes
- 1 onion
- 14 ounces (400 g) beef (a tender cut, such as tenderloin/sirloin or ribeye)
- ¼-inch (5-mm) piece ginger
- 1 clove garlic
- ½ apple
- 1 tablespoon oil
- 2½ cups (600 ml) water
- 1 (3¼-ounce/92-g) box Japanese curry sauce mix

Curry Rice

1. Cook the rice (see page 11).
2. Peel the carrots, potatoes, and onion. Cut the carrots into ¾-inch (2-cm) chunks and the potatoes into medium dice. Halve the onion and cut each half into about ¼-inch (5-mm)-thick slices. Cut the beef into 1¼-inch (3-cm)-thick slices, then into cubes. Peel and grate the ginger and garlic. Peel, core, and coarsely grate the apple (use a large-hole grater).
3. Heat the oil in a casserole and brown the meat. Add the onions and sauté over medium heat for 3 minutes. Add the carrots, apple, potato, garlic, and ginger and stir, then add the water. Cover with the lid, reduce the heat, and let cook for about 20 minutes until the vegetables are tender.
4. Cut the curry mix into small pieces and stir into the broth to color and thicken. Let cook for 5 minutes.
5. Divide the cooked rice and beef curry among four plates.

Kamome Diner

Naoko Ogigami—2006

Sachie is a single Japanese woman who is making a living in Finland by running a small restaurant. But the fact that she has not had a single customer in a month does little to dampen her resolve. We soon see her succeed as she steadily wins over the sometimes slightly lost characters who come to take refuge here for a while. The movie—with an original title that means "The Seagull Café"—revolves around the relationships gradually forged by these alternately endearing and absurd, but always cheerful and sometimes comical individuals, and their exchanges that accentuate their culture shock and stereotypes, two themes dear to its director, Naoko Ogigami. This gentle and charming comedy is classified in Japan as *iyashi-kei eiga*, a "film that provides emotional healing," typical of productions that feature peaceful lives and soothing surroundings. It makes you want to travel to Helsinki for a moment just to taste Sachie's onigiri at the Kamome Diner.

Weathering with You

Makoto Shinkai—2019

Hodaka Morishima, a young high school student, escapes his home on a remote island and heads for Tokyo. To support himself in this urban jungle, he finds work as a contributor to a magazine devoted to the paranormal and the occult. Because Japan has been experiencing a strange and unprecedented rainstorm, he is assigned to investigate the "sunshine girls," girls who are believed to be capable of controlling the weather, a legend to which he gives little credence. However, the course of his life will be changed when he meets Hina Amano, an enthusiastic and determined young girl who possesses the supernatural power to stop the rain and clear the sky. The Sunshine Girl Hina makes Hodaka her special fried rice, with the seaweed flavor of the nori shio potato chips she adds bringing out its full flavor and originality. The romance between the two teenagers, inserted into a lyrical eco-fable, is the work of director and screenwriter Makoto Shinkai, known to the general public since 2016 thanks to the international success of his animated masterpiece *Your Name*.

This famous Japanese dish, which is also known as omusubi, *comes in many variations.*

[Kamome Diner]

Serves 4 (8 rice balls)
Preparation time: 20 minutes
Cooking time: 15 minutes
Resting time: 30 minutes

Onigiri
Rice Balls

Ingredients

- 2⅓ cups (450 g) Japanese short-grain (sushi) rice
- 3 sheets nori (dried seaweed)

For the first onigiri
- 3 ounces (80 g) canned tuna in its liquid (brine)
- 1 tablespoon mayonnaise
- ½ teaspoon soy sauce
- scant ¼ teaspoon wasabi (optional)
- Salt

For the second onigiri
- 1 tablespoon katsuobushi (dried bonito flakes)
- 1 tablespoon soy sauce
- ½ teaspoon sesame oil

1. To make the first onigiri filling, drain the tuna, crumble in a bowl, and mix with the mayonnaise, soy sauce, and wasabi. Cover with plastic wrap (clingfilm) and set aside. To make the second onigiri seasoning, combine all the ingredients in a bowl.

2. To make four of the first onigiri, use the rice while still hot. Lay a square of plastic wrap on a cutting (chopping) board. Place one-eighth of the rice in the middle, spreading it with a spoon. Place one-fifth of the tuna mixture in the center, then draw all the sides of the plastic wrap together and twist the top to seal. Using your hands, press each side to form the rice into a triangle shape. Peel off the plastic wrap. Lightly season with salt. Repeat for the remaining three onigiri. Finally, coat the top of each onigiri with the remaining one fifth of the filling mixture.

3. To make four of the second onigiri, proceed as before to make four rice triangles, but use one-fifth of the onigiri seasoning on each in place of the tuna filling before covering in plastic wrap and shaping. Finally, coat the top of each onigiri with the remaining one-fifth of the mixture.

4. Cut each nori sheet horizontally into 3 strips. Attach one to the middle of each onigiri and fold the edges around. Arrange the onigiri on a serving dish.

This easy fried rice is one of the stand-out dishes made by Hina in Weathering with You.

[Weathering with You]

Serves 4
Preparation time: 10 minutes
Cooking time: 10 minutes

Ingredients

- 1 cup (100 g) button mushrooms
- 1 onion
- 4 slices ham
- 3½ cups (700 g) Steamed Rice (see page 11)
- ¾ cup (20 g) potato chips (crisps)
- 1 tablespoon soy sauce
- Vegetable or olive oil
- Salt and pepper

Extras
- Pea sprouts (toumyou) or cilantro (coriander) sprouts
- 12 potato chips (crisps)
- 4 egg yolks

Potato Chip Fried Rice with Micro Vegetables

1. Separate the stems (stalks) of the mushrooms from the caps, then dice both the stems and caps. Peel and thinly slice the onion. Thinly slice the ham. Heat the olive oil in a skillet (frying pan) and sauté the onion. Add the mushrooms, ham, rice, soy sauce, salt, and pepper. Crumble in the potato chips by hand.
2. Place one-fourth of the fried rice on a plate. Make a small well in the center of the rice and fill with an egg yolk. Repeat for the three remaining plates.
3. Sprinkle pea sprouts around the egg yolk and arrange 3 potato chips beside the rice.

The Flavor of Green Tea Over Rice

Yasujiro Ozu—1952

After being in an arranged marriage for years and without children, Taeko and Mokichi are having difficulties in their relationship, which has been reduced to the point where they have little to say to or share with each other. Because he immerses himself in his work, she calls him "obtuse"; and frustrated, she seeks the company of her friends whenever she can. When Mokichi leaves for a business trip abroad, Taeko realizes just how irreplaceable her husband is in her life. In a key, moving scene that takes place in the middle of the night, they celebrate their reconciliation by making green tea over rice together, although they have trouble finding the ingredients and utensils for making it. Despite its serious theme, this is a light and delightfully nonchalant movie, filled with humor and attention to the details of everyday life. It is a simple and genuine portrait of a Japanese couple who appear to be total opposites.

Princess Mononoke

Hayao Miyazaki—1997

In fifteenth-century Japan, the young archer Ashitaka falls victim to a curse after killing a boar god who had turned into a demon. On his quest to find the deer god who alone can free him from this spell, he is drawn unwillingly into a war being waged by San, known as Princess Mononoke, to defend the fantastic forest where she grew up, against the powerful Lady Eboshi, who rules Iron Town, a settlement that is causing destruction in the area.

This animated film features a dense plot filled with complex, varied, and unsavory characters, set in an animistic world rich in symbols. It deals with such universal themes as the relationship between humans and their environment and the escalation of violence in times of conflict, as well as the status of women, the value of work, and tolerance. This magnificent movie balances violence with poetic grandeur in the tradition of Japanese *jidaigeki*, epic period dramas.

This light, popular dish is prepared as its name ocha, "green tea," zuke, "submerged," suggests, with many possible variants and accompaniments.

[The Flavor of Green Tea Over Rice]

Serves 4
Preparation time: 5 minutes
Cooking time: 10 minutes
Resting time: overnight

Ingredients

- 2 (4-ounce/115-g) salmon fillet portions
- 4 bowls Steamed Rice (see page 11)
- ½ sheet nori (dried seaweed), torn into small pieces
- ⅕ bunch chives, minced (very finely chopped)
- 2 tablespoons toasted sesame seeds
- Wasabi (optional)
- Green tea or Dashi Broth (see page 9)

For the salmon salt solution (brine)
- scant 1 cup (200 ml) water
- 2 tablespoons fine salt
- 1 tablespoon sugar

Ochazuke

Green Tea over Rice

1. Halve the salmon fillets lengthwise and place in a plastic bag. Add the salt, sugar, and water for the salt solution (brine) and marinate overnight. Alternatively, to speed up the process, cover the salmon with 2 tablespoons fine salt and refrigerate for 15 minutes, then wash off the salt.
2. Pat dry the salmon with (kitchen) paper towels, then cook in a preheated oven at 350°F (180°C/Gas Mark 4) for 10 minutes. Remove the skin and any bones and flake the flesh with a fork.
3. Top the rice in the bowls with the salmon flakes, nori pieces, sesame seeds, and chives. Pour over hot tea or dashi broth. Serve with wasabi if desired.

This dish is the ideal combination for lovers of risotto and Japanese flavors. Use either sushi rice or risotto rice as desired.

[Princess Mononoke]

Serves 4
Preparation time: 5 minutes
Cooking time: 45 minutes
Resting time: 1 hour

Ingredients

- ¾ cup (150 g) Japanese short-grain (sushi) rice
- 4 cups (1 liter) water
- 2 teaspoons instant dashi granules
- ½ bunch chives
- 3 tablespoons (50 g) miso paste

Equipment
- Casserole or earthenware cooking pot

Japanese Risotto

1. Prepare the rice. In a bowl, wash the rice under cold running water, stir with your hand, then quickly discard the water. Repeat the operation until the water turns completely clear. Drain the rice and put into a casserole, then add the water and instant dashi granules. Let stand for 30 minutes to 1 hour until the rice turns white (it will be translucent at first).
2. Cover the casserole with the lid, place over high heat, and bring to a boil, then reduce the heat to low and simmer gently for 30 to 45 minutes.
3. When the rice is cooked, turn off the heat and stir with a wet wooden spatula. Cut the chives into about 2-inch (5-cm) lengths and mix with the rice.
4. Dissolve the miso paste in a ladle with a little hot water, then incorporate into the rice.
5. Divide among four bowls and serve immediately.

The Way of the Hot & Spicy

Various directors—2021

Sarukawa Kenta, a salesman at a beverage company in Osaka, is transferred to Tokyo. There he finds that his coworkers are in no hurry to get to know him or make him feel welcome, and he is assigned the most difficult customers. Under the influence of his new boss, Tanioka Kazuhiko, a fan of extremely spicy food, he also decides to discover the "hot & spicy." Through this gradual learning process, and thanks to his negotiating skills, he is able to significantly improve sales at the Tokyo branch and get to know his different colleagues. Each of the twenty-four episodes in this series, due to air in 2023, features an ultra-spicy dish that is unexpected and atypical in Japan, but this ploy and the tasting of each dish make the whole plot and acting all the more hilarious and endearing.

The Garden of Words

Makoto Shinkai—2013

Fifteen-year-old Takao is an apprentice shoemaker in Tokyo. Whenever he decides to skip class, this solitary daydreamer takes refuge in the Shinjuku Gyoen National Garden to sketch his shoe designs. There he meets the mysterious Yukino, a teacher twelve years his senior, who has also come to the garden to escape her professional problems. Although this is their first meeting, they have crossed paths several times, always on rainy mornings. Despite their modesty, awkwardness, expectations, and doubts, they gradually open up to each other, Takao in particular. He creates a pair of shoes for her, a symbol and metaphor in more ways than one for their growing connection. This medium-length animated film by Makoto Shinkai is beautiful and moving, always gentle and delicate, and has an incredible realism, even when immortalizing the preparation of *hiyashi chuka*, a succulent cold tomato and vegetable ramen.

Literally meaning "grilled as you like it," this Japanese savory pancake has a wide choice of toppings to suit every taste and is particularly popular in Osaka.

[The Way of the Hot & Spicy]

Serves 4
Preparation time: 15 minutes
Cooking time: 10 minutes

Ingredients

- 14 ounces (400 g) pointed cabbage (4 cups prepared)
- ¼ leek, white part only
- 7 ounces (200 g) squid (calamari)
- Vegetable oil
- 7 ounces (200 g) fresh pink shrimp (prawns), peeled
- Okonomiyaki sauce
- Mayonnaise
- Ichimi togarashi (Japanese red chili flakes)
- Jalapeño pepper paste
- 4 red chiles

For the batter
- 3¼ cups (400 g) all-purpose (plain) flour
- 1¾ cups (400 ml) cold Dashi Broth (see page 9)
- 4 eggs

Okonomiyaki
Spicy Japanese Pancake

1. Thinly slice the cabbage and leek. Clean and cut the squid into small pieces.
2. To make the batter, put the flour into a bowl, add the cold broth and eggs, and whisk to combine. Add the cabbage and leek.
3. Heat a little oil in a skillet (frying pan). Add the batter, then arrange the squid and shrimp over the top. Let cook over medium heat for about 5 minutes until golden brown, then flip. Let cook on the other side for about 5 minutes, then transfer to a plate.
4. Cover the top of the pancake with okonomiyaki sauce and mayonnaise. Sprinkle with ichimi togarashi and add a little green jalapeño paste and a red chile in the center.

Serves 4
Preparation time: 10 minutes
Cooking time: 30 minutes

This a classic of yoshoku, *the name given to Western-inspired Japanese dishes.*

[The Garden of Words]

Ingredients

- 1 cup (100 g) button mushrooms
- 1 onion
- Olive oil
- 3½ cups (700 g) Steamed Rice (see page 11)
- ½ cup (135 g) ketchup
- Salt
- Pepper

For the omelet
- 8 eggs
- ¼ cup (60 ml) milk
- 1 tablespoon sugar
- Vegetable or olive oil
- Pepper
- 1 pinch salt

Extras
- 8 cherry tomatoes
- Chopped parsley
- Baby salad leaves

For serving
- Ketchup

Equipment
Nonstick skillet (frying pan)

Omurice
Omelet Rice

1. Separate the stems (stalks) of the mushrooms from the caps, then dice both the stems and caps. Peel and thinly slice the onion. Heat olive oil in a skillet and sauté the onion. Add and sauté the mushrooms and rice, then season with salt and pepper. Add the ketchup, stir to combine, and divide the rice into four portions.

2. To make the omelet, break 2 eggs into a large bowl. Add 1 tablespoon milk, ¼ tablespoon sugar, and season with salt and pepper. Beat the mixture. Heat a little oil in a skillet over medium-high heat. Add the egg mixture. When the egg is set on the bottom but still a little runny on top, add one portion of rice across the middle. Fold both sides of the omelet over the rice. Then hold a plate under the skillet and flip the omelet onto the plate. Drizzle the top with ketchup, sprinkle with parsley, and arrange 2 cherry tomatoes and baby salad leaves on one side. Repeat the operation three more times.

映画の料理

Desserts
and Teas

These sandwiches, believed to have been invented in Kyoto in the 1920s, are a hit for Kiyo, the protagonist of The Makanai, *who combines strawberries and oranges to the delight the residents of the Maiko House.*

[The Makanai: Cooking for the Maiko House]

Ingredients

- 18 strawberries
- 4 canned peach halves
- 1 orange
- Ice cubes
- 8 slices sandwich bread
- A few mint leaves

For the whipped cream
- 1¾ cups (400 ml) heavy (double) cream (35% fat)
- 3½ tablespoons (40 g) superfine (caster) sugar

Fruit Sando

Seasonal Fruit and Whipped Cream Sandwich

1. Hull the strawberries. Cut the peach halves into quarters. Cut off both ends of the orange and peel by hand. Separate the orange sections. Peel away the membrane from the sides of each section, leaving the membrane on the outer edge in place. Place the fruit on a tray lined with (kitchen) paper towels and set aside.

2. Put a several ice cubes in a large bowl and fill halfway with water. Place a smaller bowl inside the large bowl of ice water and add the cream and sugar. Using a handheld mixer, gently whip the cream.

3. Spread the top of each bread slice with whipped cream. Set aside a little cream to cover the fruit. On one side of each sandwich, lay the fruit over the cream, arranging according to how the sandwich will be cut in half: either diagonally or in a rectangle. Cover the fruit with cream to fill in any gaps between them. Put the top half of the sandwich on the fruit, whipped cream side down. Wrap the sandwiches in plastic wrap (clingfilm) and refrigerate for 1 hour. Unwrap and halve the sandwiches in the intended direction, rinsing the knife with hot water after each cut. Cut off the crusts to reveal the fruit.

Tsurukoma's face as she savors this dessert in The Makanai *says it all! It is an original idea for completing the perfect Sunday brunch in a cozy atmosphere.*

[The Makanai: Cooking for the Maiko House]

Serves 4
Preparation time: 15 minutes
Cooking time: 35 minutes

Ingredients

- 4 slices sandwich bread
- 4 extra-large (UK large) eggs
- ⅓ cup (80 g) superfine (caster) sugar
- 2 drops vanilla extract
- 1¼ cups (300 ml) whole (full-fat) milk
- 2 tablespoons (30 g) unsalted butter, for greasing

For the caramel sauce
- 2 tablespoons superfine (caster) sugar
- 1 tablespoon room temperature water
- 1 tablespoon hot water

Equipment
- 4 gratin dishes or 1 large baking dish (¾-quart/800-ml capacity)

Bread Pudding

1. Preheat the oven to 350°F (180°C/Gas Mark 4).
2. To make the bread pudding, grease the gratin dishes or a large baking dish with butter. Cut each bread slice into small squares and line the dishes, spacing well apart.
3. Break the eggs into a medium bowl, then add the sugar and beat until incorporated. Add the vanilla and gradually incorporate the milk.
4. Pour a little of this custard mixture on top of the bread squares. Wait until the liquid is absorbed, then pour in the rest.
5. Bake on the middle oven rack for 20 to 30 minutes, until the top turns golden brown on top.
6. To make the caramel sauce, about 5 minutes before the pudding finishes cooking, put the sugar and room temperature water into a stainless steel saucepan and place over medium heat until the sugar dissolves completely, without stirring. Increase the heat to medium-high, and when the caramel begins to bubble, swirl the pan. More and more bubbles will appear as the sugar caramelizes. When the caramel turns a dark amber, remove from heat. Add the hot water to the caramel by pouring over a spatula into the saucepan (to prevent burning your hand). Continue to swirl the saucepan pan until the caramel turns very dark.
7. Drizzle the caramel sauce over the bread pudding.

One of Japan's traditional sweet dishes, this tasty soup is rich in iron and phosphorous.

[The Makanai: Cooking for the Maiko House]

Serves 4
Preparation time: 15 minutes
Cooking time: 10 minutes

Ingredients

For the mochi dumplings
- scant 1 cup (200 ml) water
- 1⅔ cups (200 g) mochi flour (sweet glutinous rice flour)

For the red bean soup
- ¾ cup (250 g) anko (sweet red bean/adzuki/azuki paste)
- 1¼ cups (300 ml) water

Oshiruko
Red Bean Soup

1. To make the mochi dumplings, combine the rice flour and water in a bowl and knead. Using your hands, shape into balls about 1¼ inches (3 cm) in diameter.
2. Cook the mochi balls in a pot of boiling water for about 3 minutes. When the dumplings float to the surface, cook for an additional 1 minute. Shock in cold water and drain.
3. To make the red bean soup. Put the anko into a saucepan and add the water. Bring to a boil, add the dumplings, and heat for 2 to 3 minutes.
4. Serve in bowls.

With its distinctive taste of grapefruit, lime, and mandarin, yuzu blends perfectly with the many virtues of kuzu, also known as kudzu or Japanese arrowroot, in this highly appreciated tea.

[Mio's Cookbook]

Serves 4
Preparation time: 2 minutes
Cooking time: 5 minutes

Ingredients

- ¼ cup (30 g) organic kuzu starch (available at health food stores) or cornstarch (cornflour)
- 3⅓ cups (800 ml) water
- ⅓ cup (80 g) yuzu marmalade, maple syrup, or honey
- Ginger slices (optional)

Yuzu and Kuzu Tea

1. Put the kuzu into a saucepan and add the water. Bring to a boil while stirring constantly with a spatula, then reduce the heat. Let cook until the liquid turns translucent. Remove from the heat and add the yuzu marmalade.
2. Serve in cups. Add a few slices of ginger if desired.

Every Day a Good Day

Tatsushi Omori—2020

The young student Noriko, whose autobiography inspired this film, was destined for a career in publishing. In a traditional house in Yokohama, she and her cousin Michiko are gradually initiated into the art of the tea ceremony. While she is dubious at first, given the slowness and countless rules involved, she discovers the soothing benefits of this painstaking tradition in the time-honored gestures of her exacting and wise teacher, Takeda. It also changes her outlook on life over the years, despite her lack of self-confidence, her doubts, and her failures. As the title explains, every day is a good day; repetition is the art of paying attention to life and its most subtle vibrations. As the protagonist learns this age-old tradition, she is invited to savor the present moment, the passing of the seasons, the brief suspension of time, in a cocoon of refinement, finesse, and delicacy that is endlessly renewed.

Sweet Bean

Naomi Kawase—2015

This movie is set in Tokyo, where Sentaro is alone running a traditional store selling dorayaki, a Japanese confection consisting of two pancakes filled with *anko*, a sweet paste made from red adzuki (azuki) beans, popularly known as *an*, the movie's original name in Japanese. Seventy-six-year-old Tokue insists on working with him and she is finally able to convince him when she lets him taste the incomparable flavor of her own recipe. Her delicious paste, made using a long and demanding process, soon brings the store success. However, the past catches up with the two protagonists, leading them in a different direction from their promise seen at the outset. This is a sensitive and moving story about rampant industrialization and the passing on of traditional know-how. It is an ode to patience and an eminently human and emotional look at the people who are left behind and the stubborn prejudices in society. The movie has also undoubtedly contributed to the recent popularity in Western countries of mochi, dorayaki, and other delicate and tasty Japanese confections.

A small and delicate confection, it is traditionally enjoyed in spring to prolong the taste of sakura, cherry blossom time, in the mouth.

[Every Day a Good Day]

Makes 8
Preparation time: 20 minutes
Cooking time: 15 minutes
Resting time: 30 minutes

Sakura Mochi

Confection to Accompany Tea

Ingredients

- ¾ cup plus 1 tablespoon (100 g) cake (Italian "00") flour
- 2½ tablespoons (30 g) sugar
- 1½ tablespoons (10 g) glutinous rice flour
- ½ cup plus 1½ tablespoons (140 ml) water
- 1 pinch organic pink food coloring
- ⅔ cup (200 g) anko (sweet red bean/adzuki/azuki paste)
- 8 salt-pickled sakura (cherry) leaves

Equipment
- Nonstick skillet (frying pan)

1. Sift the cake flour into a bowl and mix with the sugar.
2. In a separate bowl, whisk the glutinous rice flour with the water. Add the flour and sugar mixture and the food coloring, then stir the batter until smooth. Cover the bowl with plastic wrap (clingfilm) and let stand for 30 minutes at room temperature.
3. Divide the anko into 8 equal portions and shape into elongated balls.
4. Heat the skillet over low heat, then pour in 1 tablespoon batter and spread with the back of a spoon into a 4-inch (10-cm)-diameter disk. When the batter sets, flip the pancake and let cook without coloring. Remove from the pan and cover in plastic wrap to prevent it from drying out. Repeat the operation to make seven more pancakes.
5. Place a ball of anko in the middle of each pancake, then roll up the pancake and wrap with a pickled cherry leaf.
6. Serve the sakura mochi with matcha green tea.

This famous Japanese confection consists of two pancakes filled with delicious anko.

[Sweet Bean]

Makes 8
Preparation time: 15 minutes
Resting time: 15 minutes
Cooking time: 15 minutes

Ingredients

- Oil
- 1 cup plus 2 tablespoons (360 g) anko (sweet red bean/adzuki/azuki paste)

For the pancake batter
- 1⅔ cups (200 g) all-purpose (plain) flour
- 1 teaspoon active dry (fast-action dried) yeast
- 3 eggs
- ⅓ cup (80 g) superfine (caster) sugar
- 1 tablespoon honey
- ⅓ cup (80 ml) water

Dorayaki

1. To make the pancake batter, sift the flour and yeast into a bowl. In a separate bowl, whisk the eggs with the sugar until thick and pale. Gradually fold the egg mixture into the flour until smooth. Let rest for about 15 minutes. Mix the honey with the water, then stir into the batter.

2. Heat a little oil in a nonstick skillet (frying pan). Pour batter into the skillet to make disks about 3¼ inches (8 cm) in diameter and cook over very low heat. When small holes appear on the sides, flip and cook the other side for about 3 minutes. Repeat the operation to make 16 pancakes.

3. Spread 2 tablespoons anko over the middle of 8 pancakes and cover with the remaining pancakes.

It's Tough Being a Man

Yoji Yamada—1969

What is the longest-running movie series in the history of cinema to be recorded in the *Guinness Book of Records*, far ahead of the twenty-five feature-length James Bond films, for example? The answer is *Otoko wa tsuraiyo*, which translates into English as *It's Tough Being a Man*, and with fifty successive films from 1969 to 2019, this feat was achieved by a single director for the entire series. The protagonist, Torajiro Kuruma, popularly known as Tora-san, is an eccentric vagabond and traveling salesman with a foul mouth and weakness for drink. He returns to his family after decades of absence, after the death of his father has left his sister, Sakura, alone. His bad manners and clumsiness mean that he has to leave his family again, only to return to them in each new installment of the series to experience new chaos and confusion and failed romance. He is seen in each installment as a tragicomic hero who travels the country yet remains cheerful and enthusiastic. He is popular in Japan.

Kantaro:

The Sweet Tooth Salaryman

Various directors—2017

Ametani Kantaro is a sales representative for a high-end publishing company. A pastry addict, he leads a double life to satisfy his fixation with sweet treats, which means wrapping up his business appointments early so that he can indulge his sweet tooth between sales calls. This allows him to discover as many (real!) Tokyo establishments offering pastries and desserts as possible and posts about them anonymously on his blog under the username "Sweets Knight." Kabuki theater actor Onoe Matsuya plays the protagonist of this often goofy series, which features matcha Bavarian cream, hotcakes, *anmitsu*, and *ohagi*—at least twelve desserts are showcased in the twelve episodes of the first season. Every episode has Kantaro discovering a new place, and the pleasure it gives him to sample a new creation is the pretext for reveries that play out in his head, leading him to a culinary orgasm with fruit or in delirious dances under streams of syrup and cream. It is an evident nod to food porn as farcical and euphoric scenes unfold in a deliberately whimsical atmosphere.

The mochi skewer, known as dango, is a sweet and sour dessert that is popular in Japan and comes in many variations, depending on the region and the season.

[It's Tough Being a Man]

Makes 4
Preparation time: 20 minutes
Resting time: 15 minutes
Cooking time: 5 minutes

Ingredients

**For the mochi skewers
(16 mochi dumplings)**
- 1 cup (120 g) glutinous rice flour
- ½ cup (120 ml) water

For the mitarashi sauce
- scant ½ cup (100 ml) water
- 1 tablespoon cornstarch (cornflour) or potato starch
- 4 teaspoons soy sauce
- 2 tablespoons sugar

Equipment
- Nonstick skillet (frying pan)
- 4 short bamboo skewers

Mitarashi Dango

Mochi Skewers with a Soy Sauce Glaze

1. To make the mochi dumplings, combine the rice flour with the water in a bowl and knead. Using your hands, shape into balls about 1¼ inches (3 cm) in diameter.
2. Cook the mochi balls in a pot of boiling water for about 3 minutes. When the dumplings float to the surface, cook for an additional 1 minute. Shock in cold water to cool, changing the water, if necessary. Discard the water and let drain on a wire rack for about 15 minutes.
3. Thread 4 dumplings onto a bamboo skewer. Heat in a dry skillet and arrange on a plate.
4. To make the mitarashi sauce, mix the water with the cornstarch in a small saucepan and combine with the soy sauce and sugar. Place over medium heat and bring to a boil while stirring constantly with a whisk. When the sauce becomes thick and translucent, remove it from heat.
5. Drizzle the skewers with the sauce.

One episode of the Kantaro series is set in Amamidokoro Hatsune, a café specializing in traditional confectionery that offers many varieties of this red bean-based dessert.

[Kantaro: The Sweet Tooth Salaryman]

Serves 4
Preparation time: 20 minutes
Cooking time: 5 minutes
Resting time: 1 hour

Ingredients

- 4 canned peach halves
- 1 clementine
- 4 canned cherries
- 4 strawberries (optional)
- 1 kiwifruit (optional)
- 4 tablespoons anko (sweet red bean/adzuki/azuki paste)
- 1 scoop ice cream (optional)

For the kuromitsu syrup
- ½ cup packed (100 g) dark brown (muscovado) sugar
- ⅓ cup (80 ml) water

For the gelatin cubes
- 2 cups (500 ml) water
- 1½ teaspoons (4 g) agar (agar-agar) powder
- 1 tablespoon granulated sugar

Equipment
- Square mold

Anmitsu
Agar Jelly and Fruits in Syrup

1. To make the kuromitsu syrup, combine the water and brown sugar in a small saucepan. Bring to a boil over medium heat, then reduce to low. Let cook for about 5 minutes until the syrup is thick. Let cool.
2. To make the agar gelatin (jelly), combine the water, agar, and sugar in a saucepan. Bring to a boil while stirring with a whisk, then remove from heat. Pour into a square mold, let cool to room temperature, and chill for 1 hour.
3. Cut the fruits into small pieces.
4. Cut the agar gelatin into small cubes. Divide among bowls and add fruit. Place 1 tablespoon anko in the middle. Serve with kuromitsu syrup and a scoop of ice cream, if desired.

Makes 12
Preparation time: 45 minutes
Cooking time: 2 hours

Many varieties of ohagi are showcased in the Kantaro series, from traditional types, such as koshian or tsubuan, to more original ones such as apricot and vanilla.

[Kantaro: The Sweet Tooth Salaryman]

Ohagi

Glutinous Rice Balls Coated with Anko

Ingredients

- 1 cup plus 2 tablespoons (350 g) anko (sweet red bean/ adzuki/azuki paste)
- ¾ cup (50 g) shredded coconut
- 1 tablespoon matcha (green tea powder)

For the rice
- ¾ cup (150 g) glutinous (sticky) rice
- 1 cup (220 ml) water

Equipment
- Pestle

1. Cook the glutinous rice according to the directions for steamed rice (see page 11).
2. Transfer the hot rice to a bowl and mash with a wet pestle.
3. Lightly moisten your hands and shape the rice into 12 small balls. Divide the anko into 12 portions.
4. Lay a square of plastic wrap (clingfilm) on a cutting (chopping) board. Using the back of a spoon, spread a portion of anko in the middle of the plastic wrap into a disk about 4 inches (10 cm) in diameter. Place a rice ball in the center, then draw all the sides of the plastic wrap together and twist the top to seal. Mold with your palms until round. Peel off the plastic wrap. Repeat the operation to make another 11 balls.
5. Coat 4 balls in shredded coconut. Dust another 4 balls with matcha. Leave the remaining 4 balls plain.

映画の料理

Appendices

Table of contents

Alphabetical Recipe Index

Movie Index

Acknowledgments

To Marie Baumann: Thank you so much for your trust and openness, and for giving me the chance to make this adventure a reality. It gave me great pride and delight to work with you!

To Louise Agrech: Thank you for always being patient, kind, and supportive.

Thank you to everyone who worked on this book:

To David Bonnier: Thank you for the beautiful photos; they always look delicious!

To Sarah Vasseghi: Thank you for the styling and originality.

To Nicolas Beaujouan: Thank you for the sublime and often poetic graphic design.

To Sophie Greloux: Thank you for all your hard work and invaluable advice on layout and editorial matters.

To Pierre-Olivier Bonfillon: Thank you for writing the texts for the movies and series with such high quality, which confirmed and enhanced the interest of the selected Japanese films.

And last but not least, to Luc Nguyen: Thank you so much for your time and advice!

Biography

Sachiyo HARADA

Sachiyo Harada was born in Hokkaido, Japan, and graduated from the Ferrandi school in Paris, She has worked in several top restaurants. Today, she is a food stylist, cookbook author, and contributor to the Gourmet section of *Madame Figaro Japan*. She also holds culinary workshops and gives cooking classes in Paris and Tokyo.

First published in French by
Editions Gallimard Paris © Editions Gallimard, collection Hoebeke 2023
Author of movie and series texts: Pierre-Olivier Bonfillon
Movie iconography: Studio Pandora

For the English edition
© Prestel Verlag, Munich · London · New York, 2024
A member of Penguin Random House Verlagsgruppe GmbH
Neumarkter Strasse 28 · 81673 Munich

The images from the movie and series productions featured on these pages are published solely to illustrate the author's intentions.

Back cover © Image from the film *Tampopo*, directed by Juzo Itami, 1985. Courtesy of Films Sans Frontières. All rights reserved; Food photography © David Bonnier

A Library of Congress Control Number is available; a CIP catalogue record for this book is available from the British Library.

Editorial direction: Claudia Schönecker
Project management: Andrea Bartelt-Gering
Translation, copyediting, and typesetting: Cillero & de Motta for booklab, Munich
Design: Nicolas Beaujouan
Layout: Sophie Greloux
Production management: Luisa Klose
Separations: Celine Khy and Antoine Pesch www.studiob.fr (for recipe photographs) and Apex Graphic
Printing and binding: L.E.G.O., Vicenza

Printed in Italy

ISBN 978-3-7913-9321-6

www.prestel.com

PEFC/18-31-280